CW00343168

Publics and Their Health Systems

Palgrave Studies in Science, Knowledge and Policy
Series Editors: **Katherine Smith**, University of Edinburgh, UK, and
Richard Freeman, University of Edinburgh, UK

Titles include:

Sudeepa Abeysinghe
PANDEMICS, SCIENCE AND POLICY
H1N1 and the World Health Organization

Katherine Smith
BEYOND EVIDENCE-BASED POLICY IN PUBLIC HEALTH
The Interplay of Ideas

Ellen Stewart
PUBLICS AND THEIR HEALTH SYSTEMS
Rethinking Participation

Palgrave Studies in Science, Knowledge and Policy
Series Standing Order ISBN 978–1–137–39461–3 (Hardback)
(*outside North America only*)

You can receive future titles in this series as they are published by placing a
standing order. Please contact your bookseller or, in case of difficulty, write to us
at the address below with your name and address, the title of the series and the
ISBNs quoted above.

Customer Services Department, Macmillan Distribution Ltd, Houndmills,
Basingstoke, Hampshire RG21 6XS, England

Publics and Their Health Systems

Rethinking Participation

Ellen Stewart
University of Edinburgh, UK

© Ellen Stewart 2016

All rights reserved. No reproduction, copy or transmission of this publication may be made without written permission.

No portion of this publication may be reproduced, copied or transmitted save with written permission or in accordance with the provisions of the Copyright, Designs and Patents Act 1988, or under the terms of any licence permitting limited copying issued by the Copyright Licensing Agency, Saffron House, 6–10 Kirby Street, London EC1N 8TS.

Any person who does any unauthorized act in relation to this publication may be liable to criminal prosecution and civil claims for damages.

The author has asserted her right to be identified as the author of this work in accordance with the Copyright, Designs and Patents Act 1988.

First published 2016 by
PALGRAVE MACMILLAN

Palgrave Macmillan in the UK is an imprint of Macmillan Publishers Limited, registered in England, company number 785998, of Houndmills, Basingstoke, Hampshire RG21 6XS.

Palgrave Macmillan in the US is a division of St Martin's Press LLC, 175 Fifth Avenue, New York, NY 10010.

Palgrave Macmillan is the global academic imprint of the above companies and has companies and representatives throughout the world.

Palgrave® and Macmillan® are registered trademarks in the United States, the United Kingdom, Europe and other countries.

ISBN 978–1–137–46716–4

This book is printed on paper suitable for recycling and made from fully managed and sustained forest sources. Logging, pulping and manufacturing processes are expected to conform to the environmental regulations of the country of origin.

A catalogue record for this book is available from the British Library.

Library of Congress Cataloging-in-Publication Data
Stewart, Ellen, 1984–, author.
Publics and their health systems : rethinking participation / Ellen Stewart.
p.; cm. — (Palgrave studies in science, knowledge and policy)
Much of chapter 7, and several paragraphs of chapter 8, were previously published by Taylor and Francis in Critical policy studies (Vol. 9, no. 1, 2015). Much of chapter 2 was previously published by Policy Press in Policy & politics (Vol. 41, No. 2, 2013).
Includes bibliographical references.
Summary: "Drawing on a detailed case study of Scotland's National Health Service, this book argues that debates about citizen participation in health systems are disproportionately dominated by techniques of invited participation. A 'system's-eye' perspective, while often well-intentioned, has blinded us to other standpoints for understanding the complex relationship between publics and their health systems. Publics and Their Health Systems takes a 'citizen's-eye' perspective, exploring not only conventional invited participation, but also the realms of representative democracy, contentious protest politics, and the micro-level tactics used by individual citizens in their encounters with health services. The book highlights more oppositional dynamics than those which characterise much invited participation, and argues that understanding these is a crucial step towards a more inclusive and democratic health system"—Provided by publisher.!
ISBN 978–1–137–46716–4 (hardback)
I. Title. II. Series: Palgrave studies in science, knowledge, and policy.
[DNLM: 1. Consumer Participation—Scotland. 2. Health Policy—Scotland. 3. Health Planning—Scotland. WA 540 FS2]
RA987.S4
362.109411—dc23   2015025960

Typeset by MPS Limited, Chennai, India.

For Magnus and Greta

Contents

List of Figures and Tables

Figures

Tables

Acknowledgements

My thanks go, first and foremost, to everyone who has taken part in my research through interviews or allowing me to observe them in meetings. Anonymity requires that individuals are not credited with their statements in the text, but my participants' thought-provoking reflections on Scotland's health services and their relationship with them are the backbone of this book.

My interest in citizen participation was sparked by the creativity and determination I saw around me while working and volunteering for a range of charities in England and Scotland. Special mention should go to Pilton Community Health Project, where I volunteered during my PhD. My research was enriched by the wisdom and encouragement of many individuals with whom I've been lucky enough to study and work at LSE, St Andrews, and Edinburgh. Particular mention must go to Richard Freeman, Kathryn Backett-Milburn, Katherine Smith, John Clarke, Janet Newman, Sarah Cunningham-Burley, Peter Donnelly, Scott Greer, Corra Boushel, and Catherine-Rose Stocks-Rankin.

Much of Chapter 7, and several paragraphs of Chapter 8, were previously published as Stewart, E. (2015), Seeking outsider perspectives in interpretive research: young adults and citizen participation in health policy. *Critical Policy Studies* 9(2). Much of Chapter 2 was previously published as Stewart, E. (2013) A mutual NHS? The development of distinctive public involvement policy in devolved Scotland. *Policy & Politics* 41(2). My thanks to Taylor & Francis, and to Policy Press, respectively, for permission to reproduce the text here.

Chapter 6 is based on previously unpublished data from the statutory independent evaluation of the Scottish Health Board Elections and Alternative Pilots. My thanks go to the Scottish Government for permission to use the data for academic purposes, and of course to my colleagues Peter Donnelly, Scott Greer, and Iain Wilson for their agreement to use the data.

My research has been supported financially by an Economic and Social Research Council PhD studentship and a Chief Scientist Office Postdoctoral Training Fellowship. Research reported in Chapter 7 was conducted with financial and practical support from the Scottish Primary Care Research Network.

Finally, my thanks to my parents, sisters, and partner Jonny who have supported me during the writing of this book.

List of Acronyms

CHP   Community Health Partnership

GP   General Practitioner

NHS   National Health Service

NICE   National Institute for Health and Clinical Excellence

PPF   Public Partnership Forum

SNP   Scottish National Party

STS   Science and Technology Studies

1
Introducing Citizen Participation in Health Systems

There is a broadly based consensus across the political spectrum that opportunities for citizen participation should be encouraged, as both an intrinsic 'democratic' good and a route to myriad benefits, from efficient public services to more cohesive communities. This is not new; writing in 1970s America, Pateman (1976, p. 1) said that the term had become so ubiquitous that 'any precise, meaningful content has almost disappeared'. However, contemporary calls for participation differ, in important ways, from the radical demands of the 1960s and 70s. Polletta (2014, p. 457) argues that:

> participatory institutions [of the 1960s] were seen as firmly outside the establishment. Today, they are the establishment. The arguments then for participation were principled. Today, they are practical ... In an important sense, participatory democracy has gone mainstream.

This mainstream consensus on the need for, if not the means to, more participation permeates organisations in the public sector. Warren (2009a, 2009b) has argued that citizen participation initiatives are transforming the nature of contemporary democratic systems as the institutions of representative democracy struggle to retain their legitimacy, political parties drift away from their popular base, and electoral turnout falls. It is no longer seen as adequate, or even perhaps possible, for elected politicians to act as the sole conduit for public knowledge and action into the large organisations which administer and deliver public services. Across countries and in administrations across the political spectrum, these organisations have been mandated to develop, manage, and evaluate mechanisms of public participation.

1

This book takes an interpretive, critical approach to participation in health systems, an approach rooted in the work of scholars such as Wagenaar (2011), Yanow (2000, 1996) and Bevir and Rhodes (2006). It draws on research conducted in one specific (set of) institution(s), the National Health Service (NHS) in Scotland, where participation is often referred to gently as 'public involvement'. Concerns about public accountability in the UK NHS can be traced back to its creation (Hunter and Harrison, 1997; Klein and Lewis, 1976). In the early days of the NHS Bevan famously declared: 'The Minister of Health will be whipping-boy for the Health Service in Parliament. Every time a maid kicks over a bucket of slops in a ward an agonised wail will go through Whitehall' (quoted in Foot, 2009, p. 195). Since the 1970s, health policy has been concerned to establish other avenues for public redress and influence than direct control by central government. However defining the means of participation has repeatedly proved problematic for policymakers: Klein (2010, p. 234) describes the reform of public involvement policy in the UK as a 'stutteringly inconsistent process'. Proposed measures have included repeated reforms of local structures of public involvement, reforms of complaints systems, increasing local authority oversight of NHS services and, in Scotland, the direct election of members of Health Boards. However, as this chapter will demonstrate, the consistency of the criticisms and dilemmas which have plagued the various models of involvement over time is remarkable (Carlyle, 2013; Learmonth et al., 2009).

In exploring practices of participation within the Scottish NHS, this book probes fundamental tensions within current discourses of participation. These relate to the capacity of techniques of participation to generate adequate legitimacy, and to accommodate 'small-p' politics and conflict, which have a habit of spilling out of the participation initiatives that organisations plan. By filling a perceived political vacuum at the local level of the NHS (Klein and New, 1998), policies of participation have generated new political terrain, and this book is therefore simultaneously an examination of policy implementation, and of grassroots political action in both 'invited' and uninvited spaces (Gaventa, 2006). This introductory chapter reviews the current state of knowledge on citizen participation in healthcare, highlighting some of the challenges of research in the field, and then introduces the conceptual approach taken in this book.

Empirical studies of participation in health systems

Healthcare is one field where participation has been a major trend for decades (affirmed by the World Health Organization (1978) as 'a right and a duty' for citizens). However as Harrison and Mort (1998, p. 66) point out, the rhetorical ease with which participation is celebrated is not matched in practice. This is a field of academic study which has grown rapidly since the 1990s, and which is widely based across a range of health systems, with the vast majority of the literature from Europe and North America (Conklin et al., 2015). Empirical studies demonstrate a range of approaches to studying public involvement, with case studies of local initiatives (found to comprise 74% of the available literature by one systematic review (Crawford et al., 2002)) and surveys of multiple organisations the most popular approaches. However, it is a field which is increasingly acknowledged as problematic. While some studies celebrate 'successful' involvement (often, as Crawford et al. (2002) point out, in case reports authored by workers involved in projects), many others highlight difficulties and obstacles in participatory practice.

Three closely related systematic reviews of the area (Conklin et al., 2015; Crawford et al., 2002; Mockford et al., 2012) come to the same broad conclusions. Firstly, researchers have not generated adequate evidence on the *outcomes* of participation in healthcare (Conklin et al., 2015; Crawford et al., 2002; Mockford et al., 2012). Rather, a mass of often interesting case studies of implemented participatory activities document (with remarkable consistency) the process of participation. Secondly, and arguably intrinsically related to the first issue the reviews identify, studies of participation in healthcare proceed with minimal attention to the conceptual basis of the field (Conklin et al., 2015; Mockford et al., 2012). That is to say, research documents instances of practices which policymakers, practitioners, or participants consider to be 'participation', without relating this practice to a clearly articulated underpinning phenomenon of interest. In Mockford et al.'s review of public and patient involvement in the UK, 'most studies relied on, and were driven by, current policy initiatives as their primary framework' (Mockford et al., 2012, p. 35). Conklin et al., more damningly, highlighted 'the continuing absence of a consensus on the definition of public involvement, and the variation in purpose of and approaches to involvement, either of which are often not made explicit' (Conklin et al., 2015, pp. 160–161). With these linked findings as a starting point, this chapter takes an interpretive approach to discussing existing academic knowledge on citizen participation in healthcare (Greenhalgh et al., 2005). This section discusses empirical studies, while the next explores the literature's conceptual basis more thoroughly.

The absence of evidenced outcomes or 'impact' from citizen participation is a recurring, and thorny, issue within this literature, playing both to concerns that participation is merely 'tokenistic', but also that it becomes devalued as a means to an end (particularly to cost-saving or organisational efficiency goals). Entwistle (2009, p. 1) discusses the risks of instrumentalising participation for wider organisational goals, and concludes 'the notion of participation makes little sense if potential for influence is entirely lacking'. A few studies offer sympathetic interpretations of a lack of public influence through participation. In Anderson et al.'s study of London Primary Care Groups and Trusts, many of the weaknesses of public involvement exercises are attributed to a kind of complacency born of time constraints: 'Those who accepted things as they were tended to focus their energies on the mechanisms of involvement rather than the mechanisms of change – they assumed the latter were in reasonable working order' (Anderson et al., 2002, p. 61). Callaghan and Wistow's case studies of English Primary Care Groups demonstrate two different approaches to public involvement – a dialogue approach versus a snapshot – but the authors find that both are underpinned by a 'scientific rationalism' by which 'both boards gave primacy to their own "expert" knowledge' (Callaghan and Wistow, 2006, p. 2299). Some studies highlight the presence of individual staff members who promote and support involvement; Harrison and Mort (1998) describe these as 'participation entrepreneurs'. In other cases, individuals operate as a conduit for public views; Anderson et al. highlight the example of a diabetes support nurse who 'completely ignored the formal processes of decision-making and learning in the PCG but sustained a shared process of learning through her informal network of professional contacts' (Anderson et al., 2002, p. 61).

However, as Crawford et al.'s (2002) systematic review states, multiple papers conclude that staff are a crucial obstacle to the impact of involvement. Writing in the English context, Martin notes within the literature 'a widely observed reluctance on the part of health professionals and managers to engage with the public and put into practice the outputs of public-involvement processes' (Martin, 2008a, p. 1757). Harrison and Mort (1998) coin the term 'technology of legitimation' and offer an account of the way in which public involvement efforts can be used by manipulative managers:

> the simultaneous construction of user groups' legitimacy by the expression of positive views about them, and its deconstruction by reference to their unrepresentativeness and/or unsatisfactoriness as formal organisations constitutes a device by which whatever stance officials might take in respect of user group preferences or

involvement on particular issues could be justified. (Harrison and
Mort, 1998, p. 66)

In this interpretation, dilemmas of impact (attributed to staff members'
interference) are closely linked with dilemmas of representation.

Questions of representation crop up frequently within the literature
on participation in health, but are rarely satisfactorily answered. As one
review states, many studies 'had not provided an explicit definition
or statement of how the public was operationalised for the analysis
in question' (Conklin et al., 2015, p. 156). Two dimensions of representativeness tend to recur in discussion and debate about public
involvement: both can be seen as a response to the unfamiliarity of
notions of representation where a formal process of authorisation
is absent. Firstly, there is a demographic question, which Martin
describes as 'descriptive-statistical' (Martin, 2008a). This essentially
demands that representatives resemble those they represent in demographic characteristics (Pitkin, 1967). The absence of descriptive representation is, Warren (2009a) argues, a major flaw in citizen participation
initiatives, which should be resolved by methods such as random
selection of participants. A second, which is often hinted at but rarely
elaborated on in academic literature, is a simple concept of 'newness'
to civic activities; essentially one cannot be both 'ordinary' and one of
'the usual suspects'. Harrison and Mort's UK-wide study (1998) points
to the uncertain, unstable legitimacy of user groups, and to the non-
binding, informal manner in which they feed into decision-making. In
their study of NICE's Citizens Council in England, Davies et al. (2006)
identified a move away from the authority of the Council – a deliberative body founded and recruited at considerable effort and expense –
towards public opinion surveys and focus groups. Arguing that many
studies identify that 'health professionals ... keen to retain control over
decision-making, undermine the legitimacy of involved members of the
public, in particular by questioning their representativeness' (Martin,
2008a, p. 1757), Martin places the question of representativeness at the
centre of his research. However, unlike analyses which identify a zero-
sum power battle as the cause of failures, he points to ambiguity in policy objectives around involvement as creating the tension between staff
and public representatives. Reconfirming the linked nature of dilemmas
of impact and representation, in later co-authored work, Martin argues
that demands for impact or demonstrable influence should be restricted
so that a more representative sample of the population will take part
(Learmonth et al., 2009). Alternatively, one study looking at young

people in English hospitals explicitly argues for a 'listening culture', whereby issues can be raised informally, rather than formal projects of involvement (Lightfoot and Sloper, 2006). Young people, and other groups perceived as 'hard to reach', are often seen as better 'involved' through dialogue with trusted professionals, than through roles within formal mechanisms (Lightfoot and Sloper, 2006; Macpherson, 2008).

This concern with engaging 'ordinary' (Learmonth et al., 2009; Martin, 2008b) members of the public (implicitly those who do not already take part in involvement) has prompted a cluster of studies seeking public views on involvement in general (see Table 1.1). These studies include members of the public with a range of experiences, from the 'unengaged' to experienced participants. In seeking to speak for such a broad group, and in an explicit effort to move *away* from participants reflecting on their experiences, these papers are prone to broad conclusions which border on banal. Litva et al.'s article concludes simply: 'The public has much to contribute, especially at the system and programme levels, to supplement the inputs of health-care professionals' (Litva et al., 2002, p. 1825).

The recommendations offered in these four studies seeking public perspectives on participation in three different health systems are

Table 1.1 Studies of public perspectives on participation in health in general

Study	Country	Context	Method(s) used
Abelson et al. (2004)	Canada	Revising guidance for design of public involvement processes	Focus groups with experienced citizens
Litva et al. (2009)	England	Involvement in clinical governance	Focus groups with citizens with a range of experience of NHS and involvement
Litva et al. (2002)	England	Involvement in healthcare decision-making at three levels: system, programme and individual level	Focus groups and interviews with a range of the public: experienced participants to novices
Wiseman et al. (2003)	Australia	Involvement in priority setting across three levels: global, programme and between procedures	Survey of patients in waiting rooms at two medical practices

remarkably consistent. They tend to advocate a shift away from the goals of 'citizen control' (Arnstein, 1969) or 'lay domination' (Feingold, 1977), advocated by authors in the 1960s and 1970s. Thus Litva et al. (2009) promote 'overseeing' as an alternative to control. Wiseman et al. support partnership and collaboration:

> Citizens in this study felt that they have a legitimate role to play in priority setting in health care but that this role must be a joint one involving other groups, namely clinicians, health service managers, and patients and their families. (Wiseman et al., 2003, p. 1010)

Litva et al. (2002) broadly concur, noting that citizens may be wary of having the final say. The desire to access an 'ordinary' perspective on participation has prompted these authors to broaden analysis away from case studies of practice, eliciting generalised 'public' perspectives on participation through focus groups and surveys. These advocate 'weaker' forms of participation, and a move away from the goal of citizen control.

Overall, empirical studies of public involvement in health since the late 1990s have had a consistent and closely linked set of findings. They have repeatedly found problems and inadequacies in the practice of participation in health, often revolving around the challenges of balancing concerns about (demographic) representation and the need to demonstrate impact on structures and services (Learmonth et al.'s (2009) 'catch 22'). Something of a consensus has developed that participation should be 'embedded' into services in order to channel the views of as wide a range of the public as possible, even at the risk of sacrificing the goal of citizen control (Litva et al., 2009; Tritter, 2009; Tritter and McCallum, 2006). In the next section, we will explore the conceptual understandings of participation which frame these findings.

The conceptual basis of research on participation in health systems

Stating the indeterminacy of the concept of participation has become something of a lynchpin of introductory sections (Bishop and Davis, 2002; Bochel et al., 2008; Conklin et al., 2015; Crawford et al., 2002; Tritter, 2009). However, the literature has continued to grow apace, revolving around a range of compounds formed by adding a named group of participants ('public', 'patient', 'citizen', or 'user') to a type of activity ('involvement', 'engagement', or 'participation'). The result is literature that shares a family resemblance (Wittgenstein, 1953) rather than a terminological grounding. One editorial for a 'virtual special issue' on public participation in health describes searching the archives of the journal *Social Science and Medicine*: 'each of the search terms "public" and "community" was combined with each of the terms "participation, engagement, deliberation and involvement"' (Tenbensel, 2010, p. 1). By and large this curious instability – resulting in what Rowe and Frewer (2005, p. 252) describe as 'synonyms of uncertain equivalence' – is given little attention within the literature. As one paper puts it, with little explanation, 'involvement will be considered as a generic term that encompasses the notions of participation, consultation and engagement' (Wait and Nolte, 2006, p. 152). Other papers choose an alternative umbrella concept and consider involvement as a subset (Rowe and Frewer, 2005). Perhaps the most common response to this discursive instability is to shift repeatedly and without explanation between different terms. As an illustrative example, O'Keefe and Hogg (1999) use 'public participation' in their title, select 'user involvement' as a keyword, 'public involvement' in their abstract, and in the body of the article shift apparently arbitrarily between 'community involvement', 'user involvement', 'public involvement', 'user participation', and 'community participation' (with the titular term 'public participation' neither defined nor used thereafter). Occasionally trends emerge whereby certain terms become particularly common in specific contexts or periods. For example, 'patient and public involvement' as an analytic category seems to be a predominantly UK-based construction associated with New Labour policy of the late 1990s and 2000s (Forster and Gabe, 2008).

The key tactic of authors struggling with the indeterminacy of the concept of participation has been to refer to a series of typologies of participation which have developed in the wake of Arnstein's (1969) 'ladder of participation'. As highlighted by Kuhn's (1962) account of normal science, a specific set of approaches to a given research topic becomes standard practice, limiting its analytic and critical potential. This leads to recurring themes within the literature and unquestioned approaches and definitions: the ubiquity of typologies of participation can be seen as just such an approach. Typologies are more generally acknowledged to 'be seductive in their capacity to simplify thought' (Weiss, 1994, p. 174). In the participation in healthcare literature this tendency is closely linked to definitional struggles; typologies have been one way to deal with the wide range of initiatives that profess to be 'participation'.

Table 1.2 sets out five typologies of public involvement from the literature which all concern themselves with defining the 'level' of involvement. Crucially, what is categorised within these typologies is an assessment of the degree of power gained by citizens, the public, or specific service users. Thus, they offer not forms or practices of involvement, but summative evaluations of activities. While other authors have added the further dimension of 'role' (whether user or citizen) (Charles and Di Maio, 1993; Harrison et al., 2002), level is the more consistent feature. Many, if not most, articles on the topic reference at least one of those featured in Table 1.2. There is significant consistency in placement. Typologies can be easily mapped against each other, and even where the actual descriptor changes, the content of the 'level' (as defined by each author) is reasonably consistent. Essentially, most are predicated on an increase in public power from top to bottom, with the exception of Rowe and Frewer (2005), who claim to construct their framework on the basis of information flows (from 'sponsor' to public, from public to 'sponsor', and between 'sponsor' and public). Involvement, engagement and participation sometimes appear as the umbrella concept, and sometimes as one level of an alternative concept.

Two points are worth making about Table 1.2. Firstly, over time, typological levels have tended not just to reduce in number (as a straightforward simplification of Arnstein's (1969) typology), but to concentrate in the middle of the ladder. Although in contemporary literature these early typologies appear merely descriptive, they grew out of a 'paradigmatic phase' (Kuhn, 1962) which sought to critique specific instances of involvement. Initial papers in the 1960s and 70s came out of community activism and community development in the USA; they are highly normative, provocative, and action-oriented (Arnstein, 1969; Feingold, 1977). Thus Arnstein's (1969) influential typology aimed to uncover not merely tokenistic activities (a common goal in later studies), but even more malign manipulative and 'therapeutic' acts (the latter resonating with Edelman's (1974) critique of the 'helping professions'). Feingold's (1977) chapter, which sought to amend Arnstein's framework for health-specific contexts, argues that the community can join forces with administrators to oppose professional power.

Therapy, manipulation, and the aspirational inclusion of citizen control, all fall away in more recent literature. The concentration of typologies in an uncontroversial middle range of activities is likely connected to broader sociological shifts into what Scambler and Britten (2001, p. 46) call a 'post-conflict' phase. In periods where it is unfashionable

Table 1.2 Typologies of 'level' of participation

Author	Arnstein	Feingold	Charles and Di Maio	Rowe and Frewer	Martin
Year	(1969)	(1977)	(1993)	(2005)	(2009)
Concept	'citizen participation'	'citizen participation'	'lay participation'	'public engagement'	'public engagement'
Levels	Manipulation				
	Therapy				
	Informing	Informing		Communication	Information
	Consultation	Consultation	Consultation	Involvement	Consultation
	Placation				
	Partnership	Partnership	Partnership	Participation	Co-production
	Delegated power	Delegated power			
	Citizen control	Citizen control	Lay domination		

to emphasise conflicts of interest between medical services and their patients, the possibilities of conflict and domination within healthcare are downplayed. The rejection of a more radical critique of contemporary participation also reflects increasing reliance on research funding for commissioned research (Scambler, 2001). In England, a critical mass of research commissioned by the English Department of Health in the late 1990s sought to inform policy implementation (for a summary, see Farrell, 2004). This literature is highly applied, and concerned primarily to improve practice within the frame of existing policy. Conceptual questions are neglected in favour of more 'useful' practical conclusions, and typologies are referenced in passing, in lieu of a statement of conceptual intent. As the provocative content of early typologies has been excised, we are left with a framework that lacks the radical potential of its forebears.

Secondly, the enduring appeal of these typologies is problematic because of the way that it neglects documenting practice in favour of forming a summative judgement; these typologies are simply inadequate for the basic conceptual job of 'fact-storing and fact-containing' (Sartori, 1984). The central concern of each typology is to determine how empowering any given instance of involvement is, and thus these ostensibly descriptive devices actually rest on a normative assessment. Having these as a starting point masks some fundamental disagreements about the basic question of what 'counts' (and crucially, does not 'count') as participation. At least two distinct understandings are present within the literature. Most papers focus on participation as a governmental or organisational action (albeit one which creates opportunities for public action). Many papers explicitly or implicitly identify public involvement as something to be found in policy documents; an exhortation to staff: 'a succession of policy initiatives designed to make the NHS more aware of patient views, more sensitive to consumers and more accountable to the public' (Klein, 2004, p. 207). Alternatively, Andersson et al. introduce it as something akin to an ethos, or perhaps a toolkit of approaches: 'a number of ways of working that all share a commitment to involving the public' (Andersson et al., 2006, p. 9). By contrast, other authors discuss participation as a naturally occurring, out-there phenomenon, leading to definitions such as 'ways in which patients can draw on their experience and members of the public can apply their priorities to the evaluation, development, organisation and delivery of health services' (Tritter, 2009, p. 276), and 'the active participation in the planning, monitoring, and development of health services of patients, patient representatives, and wider public as potential patients' (Crawford et al., 2002, p. 1). Other papers simply employ both understandings: Anton et al. (2007) introduce public involvement as governmental action and then include bottom-up action as the analysis proceeds.

The literature on citizen participation on health is thus built on unstable terrain with little shared conceptual foundation. Cursory reference to Arnstein and her successors distracts us from these more foundational questions. This makes the task of understanding 'what participation actually does' (Braun and Schultz, 2010) both more urgent, and more difficult. As several others have argued, it may be time to stop refining these summative typologies and instead attempt to produce fuller understandings of the practice and consequences of par-ticipation. For Contandriopoulos (2004, p. 328) 'public participation is only that indistinct and undefined part of normal political and admin-istrative behaviours we are used to calling that way'. Building on this inclusive, pragmatic definition, this book aims to uncover and explicate the multiple strands of intention and practice contained within the contemporary phenomenon of citizen participation in health.

A citizen's-eye view: modes of participation

The sections above illustrate the conventional parameters through which academic study of participation in health systems has been approached. There are problematic areas of neglect or omission, but there is also a wealth of knowledge and interest. The sheer volume of material stands testament to the enduring interest and importance of questions of participation in health. However, as a consequence of a shift from critical studies 'of' policy towards applied, technically minded studies 'for' policy, debates on participation in healthcare have become stuck in the system standpoint of organisations seeking to operationalise, and crucially, to document evidence of, participation. This has, Lehoux et al. note, entailed a focus 'on the processes that could be deployed and on the selection criteria that would enable picking up the right participants given their level of expertise and/or detachment vis-à-vis the issues under discussion' (Lehoux et al., 2012, p. 1849), at the expense of careful understanding of the perspectives of citizens both outside, and inside, these processes. Where 'uninvolved' perspectives have been sought, through focus groups and surveys, they have too often been elicited within a policy frame in which 'the language of policy and action ... often masks or distorts a service user perspective' (Huby, 1997, p. 1159). It is difficult to establish critical space for analysis when current government policy is used to define the phenomenon of interest.

When beginning my empirical research in this area the narrowness of conceptual accounts of participation was highlighted by a hard-won series of interviews about 'public involvement' with young adults in one Scottish community, discussed in Chapter 7. Having struggled to recruit interviewees, I drove home from interview after interview feeling disheartened at my failure to elicit the perspectives I needed to hear. There seemed to be a lacuna at the heart of my research. However, my interviews were not lacking in content. My interviewees all spoke to me, some of them at length, about their experiences of using, and acting within, health services and their community. The problem was not a lack of data, but the mismatch between this data and the analytic categories with which I had entered the field. Holding onto a particular vision of participation was blinding me to the richness of my data. What's more, this vision of participation was sharply coloured by a debate which had been generated by academics and policymakers, and bore no relevance to an interviewee sitting worrying about some aspect of their body or mind.

One major consequence of the system-oriented approach to understanding participation is a near-total disconnect between discussion of invited and uninvited modes of participation. Writing on concept misformation, Sartori identified this risk as long ago as 1970:

> Participation means self-motion ... so conceived, participation is the very opposite, or the very reverse, of mobilisation. Mobilisation does not convey the idea of individual self-motion, but the idea of a malleable, passive collectivity which is being put into motion at the whim of persuasive – and more than persuasive – authorities ... [P]articipation is currently applied by the discipline at large both to democratic and mobilisational techniques of political activation. (Sartori, 1970, p. 1051)

The notion of a distinction between invited and uninvited forms of participation is a reasonably familiar one within the wider participation literature (Gaventa, 2006; Wynne, 2007). Within the healthcare literature it occasionally appears in passing references: Abelson (2001, p. 791) distinguishes 'routine, solicited participation as compared to unsolicited, issue-driven participation'. However, when it comes to time to formalise our picture of participation in health into a typology, or taxonomy, or some other visual representation, an organisational perspective tends to prevail, and the presence of uninvited participation falls away. This has consequences for the extent to which we acknowledge or even see the ways in which publics proactively seek to shape their health systems, or at least their own interactions with those systems. Starting instead from the perspective (or standpoint) of publics directs our attention towards a wider range of engagements between citizens and system, and, I argue, makes some of the claimed distinctions between different invited technologies of participation appear less distinct and less relevant.

In this book I delineate five distinct 'modes of participation' for interactions between publics and their health systems: three invited (committee work, outreach projects, and representative democracy) and two uninvited (protests and campaigning, and subversive service use). It is worth clarifying what these 'modes of engagement' are and are not. These are not types of public; it is possible, indeed likely, that most modes are populated by many of the same people (possessed of resources of time, confidence, connections, and skills) while a 'silent majority' takes little or no action. There is nothing to say that a working class young adult might not become a consummate and expert activist, nor that a retired professional might not choose to use services subversively. I suspect there are demographic clusters within particular modes, but do not propose that these be used as defining or identifying characteristics of them. The modes are also not specific actions (e.g. protest, vote) available to members of the public, because, particularly in the case of the invited modes, they tend to require some input from the organisation in question. I understand them more as moments of interaction in which there is potential for public action.

There is overlap with the conventional policy tools which policymakers reach for to mandate participation; what I describe as a 'policy toolbox' in Chapter 2. However there are also important differences, both in what will never make it into the toolbox (for example, the idea of creating situations in which citizens organise marches to protest a decision), and in what is in the toolbox, but in a fundamentally altered form (for example, the difference between explicit, incentivised patient choice in a provider quasi-market, and secretive, tacit choices between individual health professionals in a given GP surgery). While the 'policy toolbox' is an attempt to specify the full range of options available, the modes of engagement discussed are not; these are the modes inductively theorised from my empirical data. Nor are these modes a menu from which members of the public can straightforwardly select their 'best' tactic.

In Chapter 8 I argue that the selection of a particular mode depends on more than an assessment of how likely a given course of action is to yield power, or advance an individual's self (or group) interest. Rather it reflects individually held, and perhaps rarely articulated knowledge: about the organisation with which one seeks to engage; about one's place (or lack of) within that organisation; and about the communities in which one exists.

This book thus emphasises questions about the boundaries of what participation means within health systems, and pays notably less attention to questions about what the terms 'citizen', 'publics', or 'the public' mean. Baggott (2005) offers an excellent summary of the challenges of defining the appropriate constituency, and using the 'right' terminology in this area of policy and analysis. Across the chapters I present data from interviews with top NHS managers, elected councillors, Health Board non-executive directors, retired professionals volunteering their time to sit on committees, and a group of young adults, including a recovering heroin addict, a recent graduate in their first job, and a young parent looking after children at home. These individuals are all, of course, part of the public, and the book thus operates with an inclusive, eclectic definition in which I do not seek to distinguish and neatly label 'ordinary members of the public' from existing participants or NHS 'insiders'. Lehoux et al. (2012) argue that participatory processes often implicitly or explicitly seek out a disinterested participant who lacks the 'sociological concreteness of citizens'. In undertaking qualitative research, particularly in-depth interviews, which seek to create space for research participants to explore and discuss, I endeavour to understand participation as perceived and practiced by 'real people'. These 'real people' are part of multiple, contingent, and shifting 'publics'. This links with a literature which has tried to problematise the notion of an out-there 'public' awaiting representation:

> This assumes a singular and reflective voice – rather than a heteroglossic, and potentially conflicted, view of potential or emergent publics. Ideas of 'summoning' or 'convening' publics point to the political work of imagining potential 'we's' and findings ways of inviting or recruiting them. (Newman and Clarke, 2009, p. 182)

Structuring this book around modes of participation seeks to place everyday, situated, embodied human action centre-stage.

data and methods

of public action presented in this book draws on empirical
lected and analysed by the author (in some cases working
with colleagues) in Scotland between 2009 and 2014, across three distinct projects.

1. The mainstay of the book is my ESRC-funded doctoral research
   (grant number ES/F023405/1), data collection for which took place
   in 2009–2010. As well as extensive desk-based research into policy
   frameworks, I undertook data collection in a Community Health
   Partnership which I call Rivermouth. This interpretive project
   explored three different sets of perspectives on local practices of
   public involvement (those of staff, of public participants, and of
   'unengaged' 18–25 year olds) by way of semi-structured interviews,
   documentary analysis, and observation of meetings. The methodology for this research is reported more fully in Stewart (2012, 2013).
   Ethical approval for this research was granted by the University of
   Edinburgh School of Social and Political Science Ethics Committee.
   The Scotland A committee of the NHS Medical Research Ethics
   Committee confirmed that the project constituted 'service evaluation', and therefore did not require full NHS ethics approval.
2. I have also been pleased to be granted permission to re-use data
   from the Scottish Government-funded independent evaluation of
   the Scottish Health Board Elections (and Alternative Pilots) study
   which I worked on from 2010 to 2012 with Professor Peter Donnelly,
   Dr Scott Greer and Dr Iain Wilson. This ambitious project involved
   extensive data collection in four Health Board Areas, including observation of Board meetings, a quantitative survey of voters and candidate, and interviews with several hundred Board members, staff and
   stakeholders. The official reports of this study are available (Greer
   et al., 2011, 2012) and the research is reported in a range of academic journals (Greer et al., 2014a, 2014b; Stewart et al., 2014, 2015;
   Wilson et al., 2015). Ethical approval for this research was granted by
   the University of St Andrews Medical School Teaching and Research
   Ethics Committee.
3. Finally, some of the data discussed in Chapter 5 was collected in
   2014 as part of my Chief Scientist Office-funded postdoctoral fellowship (grant number PDF/13/11) on public engagement and evidence
   use in hospital closure processes. This was collected in desk-based
   research, and ethical approval for this research was granted by the

University of Edinburgh Centre for Population Health Sciences Research Ethics Sub-group.

My analysis draws on policy documents (both local and national) and extensive non-participant observation of meetings of Scottish Health Boards, Board committees and Public Partnership Forums. However, the mainstay of the book is data from upwards of 100 semi-structured qualitative interviews with NHS staff and members of the public across Scotland. Interviewees were usually selected as 'key informants', with the exception of my young adult interviewees; an account of that recruitment process is given in Chapter 7.

My interpretive approach is strongly shaped by a commitment to studying localised experiences and perceptions. Much of the literature on citizen participation moves quickly from empirical findings to abstract typologies and recommendations for improvement; 'the normative slides uneasily into the descriptive' (Mahony et al., 2010, p. 2010). In studying both 'publics' and 'participation' I seek to avoid what Smith (2001) describes as 'nominalising' verbs into nouns: 'when the activities of individuals communicating, organising, and informing become abstracted into "communication", "organisation" and "information"' (Meuleman and Boushel, 2014, p. 51). These 'grammatical forms ... repress the presence of people as agents' (Smith, 1999, p. 39). Following Soss's (2006, p. 132) 'practice-centred view of interviewing for interpretive research', in this book I prioritise scepticism about shared meaning; foreground my interviewees' own sense-making; and seek to understand their behaviour as reasonable. All interview quotes are anonymous: where names are given these are pseudonyms. Where interviewees spoke in local Scottish vernacular, I have retained this rather than translate into formal English. An explanation of unusual words is given in square brackets within the text.

Conclusion

The structure of the book is as follows. Chapter 2 offers a comprehensive introduction to public involvement policy in Scotland since devolution, analysing policy documents to elucidate the evolving approach to public involvement in the country. Chapters 3–7 present empirical data from the research described above, with each chapter considering a different mode of participation in the Scottish NHS. Chapter 3 focuses on 'lay' representation on committees, and on specific standalone public committees. Chapter 4 explores health system information-gathering via what I group together as 'outreach' activities. Chapter 5 presents an analysis of the participation opportunities generated when structures of representative democracy have been brought into the Scottish NHS. Chapters 6 and 7 then turn to uninvited action: Chapter 6 takes the example of public protests against hospital closure and Chapter 7 explores what I describe as 'subversive service use' among a group of young adults. In Chapter 8 I draw together the modes I have discussed, explore how they may interact, and attempt to map their key characteristics to offer a framework to understand a range of relationships between publics and their health systems. While the key structuring device of the book is thus how publics act within health systems, Chapter 8 also seeks to draw our focus away from a behaviourist analysis of individual decision-making and towards a critical analysis of how health systems construct and shape the spaces within which publics variously enlist, resist, and subvert.

Authors in the evidence-based medicine-oriented field of health services research (Greenhalgh, 1999) continue to seek clearer, more specific, and less refutable evidence of 'what works' for organisations 'doing' participation (Abelson and Gauvin, 2006). As one of the systematic reviews discussed above put it, 'we were less interested in what is generally known, or not, and more concerned to learn about what was reported to "work", with what effect(s) and the nature of this evidence' (Conklin et al., 2015, p. 2). By contrast, in other disciplines, more ostensibly modest but potentially far-reaching efforts to understand participation are under way. Braun and Schutz (2010, p. 403), writing from a public understanding of science perspective, call for scholars to 'develop a critical inventory of the forms, formats and methods of public participation and to examine and discuss their respective implications and ambiguities'. By exploring practice across a specific health system, I seek to problematise the approaches to citizen participation that currently dominate the topic. Offering a new perspective on the cluttered field of participation in healthcare requires that such an inventory acknowledge a far wider range of publics and public action than has hitherto been the case.

2
Scotland's NHS: Citizen Participation and Mutuality in Scottish Health Policy

Introduction

In Chapter 1 I introduced the subject of participation in healthcare in international contexts. Throughout this book I work with empirical material from the Scottish NHS as a case study of how participation has been attempted in practice, across one health system. This is not because Scotland is an outlier, taking a particularly radical, effective (or indeed, ineffective) approach to the challenges of 'doing' participation. It is partly a function of the unusual breadth of empirical data I accumulated (working alone, or with colleagues) in Scotland between 2009 and 2014, ranging from interviews with 'ordinary' citizens and frontline staff to senior civil servants and managers. However, it is also an intellectual choice, because in the 15 years since devolution, the Scottish health system had been in an unusual state of flux, in which the path dependency which shapes so much of day-to-day policy in most health systems (Greener, 2002) was, if not negated, at least called into question. As successive administrations have sought to define a way forward for the NHS in Scotland (and in the case of the Scottish National Party administrations from 2007 onwards, to define a way forward which breaks with the past and current status quo elsewhere in the UK) an eclectic and at times downright contradictory set of policy tools as evolved. Accordingly, the Scottish case allows us to explore lay representatives within bureaucracy, outreach to the ever-elusive 'ordinary' citizen, and experiments with introducing representative democracy to the NHS.

This chapter begins by introducing Scottish health policy, with a particular focus on how it has been researched since devolution in 1999. I then introduce the notion of a 'policy toolbox' for participation in health, before presenting an analysis of the policy tools within public involvement policy in Scotland since devolution. I conclude by arguing that the eclecticism of this selection of tools makes Scotland a useful case study of practices of participation in healthcare.

The study of Scottish health policy

Healthcare policy is the archetypal example of post-devolution distinctiveness across the four nations of the UK. Unlike education (Arnott and Ozga, 2010; McPherson and Raab, 1988) and criminal justice (McAra, 2008), health policy in Scotland was broadly consistent with that in England until devolution. At devolution, health was one of the areas fully devolved to the Scottish Parliament. Rather than a traditional federal system, what has emerged is a system where Edinburgh has a high degree of autonomy in policy-making (Keating, 2010), with formal contact between Edinburgh and Whitehall conducted on the basis of Joint Ministerial Committees (Greer and Trench, 2010). Contrasting this with the system of parallel ministries at federal and state level in Germany, the USA, and Canada, Keating remarks that for much UK policy 'there is now no "centre" at all' (Keating, 2002, p. 5). Factors constraining divergence include the continued financial dependence of Scotland on Westminster via block grant funding (Parry, 2002) and the continued UK control of issues such as professional regulation and the remuneration of health service employees (Greer and Trench, 2010). Nonetheless, the structures of the NHS in Scotland and England now look remarkably different. The English NHS has been subject to repeated structural reorganisations and the extension of competition (Katikireddi et al., 2014) while north of the border a re-elected SNP administration defends the system of unified territorial Boards (in place since 2005) and the rejection of private provision of health services. Thus, while the NHSs in Scotland and England both remain tax-funded, state-governed health systems, there are far fewer structural similarities than at any point since 1948.

The study of devolved Scottish health policy is still young, but its birth into the midst of a heavily politicised debate about devolution, and, more recently, independence (Bennet, 2014), has complicated its development. Studies of Scottish health policy since devolution have been preoccupied with the question of divergence from previous or current UK policies. This is not particular to health policy: education policy in Scotland has always been different from that in England, and self-consciously so. McPherson and Raab (1988) discuss the extent to

which the 'assumptive worlds' (Vickers, 1965) of the Scottish education policy community have been ordered by myths about the tradi-
tions of Scottish social democracy; 'a theory supported by data it had
helped to create' (McPherson and Raab, 1988, p. 499). The health
policy community in Scotland can be seen as similarly beguiled by
Scottish distinctiveness. In interviews with public health stakeholders
and practitioners, Harrington et al. found explicit rejection of England's
marketised approach and approval of a perceived Scottish ethos of
collaboration: 'This emphasis on differences in the "ethos" between
countries recurred frequently in the Scottish interviews' (Harrington
et al., 2009, p. e27).

Greer's (2004) four-nation study can be seen as the founding text
of the study of post-devolution Scottish health policy. He proposes
an attractively straightforward characterisation of the 'trajectories' of
health policy in the four nations since devolution and considers the
devolution settlement as a 'divergence creation machine'. For Greer,
Scotland's health policy 'bets on professionals as the state's allies in
providing effective, efficient, legitimate health care and health care
rationing. The logic, if not the forms, are close to the 1974 NHS – and
the criticisms are the same as well' (Greer, 2004, p. 63). Explicitly comparative studies such as this (and that offered by the British Medical
Association (2007)) set the tone for the narratives offered by textbook
accounts of post-devolution Scotland. Keating (2010) and Tannahill
(2005) offer overviews of Scottish health policy imbued with concern
for its post-devolution distinctiveness. They describe a selection of
'headline' shifts (for example, the smoking ban) which demonstrate
'the Scottish Executive's ability to take a different legislative stance
to that south of the border' (Tannahill, 2005, p. 209). The analyti-
cal selection of these 'headlines' is rarely problematised. It is unclear
whether their significance is primarily political, or is based on some
academic standard of policy significance. Birrell (2009, p. 35) identifies
flagship policies as either possessing an assessed level of innovation or
as self-identified as such by governments. McGarvey and Cairney use
the term in a more exclusively political sense to refer to 'legislation ...
which is perhaps not only high profile but also a symbol of intent'
(McGarvey and Cairney, 2008, p. 205).

This 'current consensus' (Smith et al., 2009, p. 218) on a distinctive
Scottish approach to health policy has met some opposition (Mooney
and Poole, 2004; Mooney and Scott, 2005). Prior et al.'s (2012) inci-
sive analysis cites Freud's (1961) 'narcissism of minor differences', and
highlights the commonalities in health policy across the four nations.

Taking this point even further, other empirical research suggests that 'Seemingly sharp national level policy differences appear to have limited importance as determinants of how each system provides access to elective services and how these services are experienced by patients' (Peckham et al., 2012, p. 215).

My concern in this book is not to contribute to an assessment of Scottish difference from English, Welsh, or Northern Irish policy, but to offer a detailed study of the development of one area of policy and practice in Scotland since devolution. It is my contention that debates around post-devolution policy divergence have created a somewhat polarised picture of policy which identifies grand characterisations of the entire health system ('professionalistic' 'collaborative') and particular decisions (free prescriptions, Health Board elections), while neglecting the middle order accounts of policy that link them. In focusing on the example of participation in health, this chapter aims to offer an account of policy at this middle range.

The policy toolbox for participation in health

Chapter 1 described how research on participation in health is increasingly framed by current policy initiatives, rather than transparent conceptual frameworks (Mockford et al., 2012). One consequence of this is that the literature has not developed a systematic analysis of the policy instruments of participation over time and space; how policymakers have sought to effect 'public involvement' across health systems.

In an overview of the policy options for democracy and accountability in the UK NHS, Hunter and Harrison (1997, pp. 138–150) set out eight possibilities, including: elected local authority members on health boards; fully elected health boards; elected board chairs; health services coming under local authority control; a national set of healthcare rights; patient choice of provider; strengthened local structures of involvement and oversight (such as Community Health Councils); and improved complaints procedures. These are specific to UK (even English) structures at the time, and the inclusion of patient choice of provider reflects the authors' interest in consumerism, and the contemporaneous interest in patient choice in health policy debates (Greener, 2009; Le Grand, 2007). My concern with *publics* and their health systems, rather than Hunter and Harrison's *consumers*, makes this particular policy tool less relevant. Nonetheless the chapter offers a useful, if rarely elaborated, 'menu' which illustrates some of the key possibilities in reshaping public roles within the governance of health systems.

Drawing on this, and the wider international literature, we can construct a typology of the key policy instruments by which participation is developed within health systems:

- Strengthening links between existing structures of representative democracy and healthcare organisations, or introducing new structures of representative democracy within healthcare organisations.
- Strengthening structures for individual citizens to assert themselves as service users (e.g. enforceable healthcare rights; public complaints mechanisms).
- Requiring either healthcare organisations or independent actors to conduct (research-style or democratically inspired) outreach projects to gather views from the public.
- Inviting members of the public onto existing committees and/or creating standalone forums and committees for citizens to oversee work of healthcare organisations.

This list can be understood as the notional 'toolbox' from which policymakers choose their tools: the structural limitations of publicly funded health systems mean that there are only a limited number of options for attempting to enhance citizen participation. Actual choices will, of course, reflect the widely acknowledged path dependency of policymaking (Greener, 2002).

Examples of these four tools for participation can be seen across different health systems internationally. Links with representative democracy are perhaps archetypally found in New Zealand's elected Health Boards (Laugesen and Gauld, 2012) and similar models elsewhere, including several Canadian provinces (Stewart et al., 2015). However, the 'Nordic model' of local authority control of health services (Martinussen and Magnussen, 2009) is an important alternative model which shares a commitment to the legitimacy of representative democratic techniques over alternatives modes of public accountability. England's Patient Advice and Liaison Service (Heaton et al., 2007; South, 2007) and formalised complaints processes in, *inter alia*, England (Allsop and Jones, 2008) and Canada (Beardwood et al., 1999) are examples of policy seeking to harness (negative) service user experiences to improve the system. The extent to which these processes individualise negative experiences (in what Beardwood et al. (1999) identify as a defensive, legalistic way) may limit the 'publicness' of these policy tools. By contrast, outreach projects, ranging from ambitious events such as 2014's NHS Citizen Assembly in England (The Tavistock Institute et al., 2014), to the modest client surveys described in Australian primary care (Freeman et al., 2014) have the potential to create space for a wider range of service user experience, and are more explicitly focused on system improvements than individual redress. Finally, and perhaps most widely discussed in the academic literature, policymakers have often either created standing committees of 'lay people' to oversee or advise decision-makers (such as Community Health Councils, Public and Patient Involvement Forums, and Local Involvement Networks in England (Baggott, 2005; Gibson et al., 2012)) or have encouraged the inclusion of designated 'lay representatives' on existing committee structures, sometimes to represent specific groups such as the Maori population in New Zealand (Boulton et al., 2004). In the next section I explore the presence and absence of these policy tools in Scottish health policy since devolution.

Scottish health policy and the participation toolbox

Participation is a particularly pertinent field of health policy in the post-devolution Scottish context. In rejecting the choice and competition model influential in England since 2002, Scottish health policy has been described as 'professionalistic' (Greer, 2004) or in the BMA's more flattering characterisation, focused on 'collaboration and integration' (BMA Health Policy and Economics Research Unit, 2010). A unified territorial Board structure minimises opportunities for dissatisfied patients to exit, except to move between primary care practices, and this has pushed public involvement high on the policy agenda.

To ground the empirical chapters which follow, this section draws on a qualitative analysis of Scottish health policy documents published between 2000 and 2007. Analysis of policy documents has been somewhat neglected in studies of policy divergence in the UK post-devolution, which have tended to rely predominantly on interviews with national level policymakers and stakeholders (Greer, 2004) or on legislative output (Keating et al., 2003). Policy documents can offer another useful perspective because, if we assume that Scottish distinctiveness is embedded into the 'assumptive worlds' (Vickers, 1965) of policymakers, it is incumbent on researchers to go beyond interview self-reports of a national policy 'ethos'. The particular value of this approach is in supporting analysis more detailed than macro accounts and yet more contextualised than 'flagship' decisions. Smith et al., drawing on the work of Freeman (2006), argue that policy documents 'frame the nature of public policy problems, shape the boundaries of possible responses and act as points of reference for a wide variety of actors to justify subsequent positions' (Smith et al., 2009, p. 219).

In this section I analyse four health White Papers published between 2000 and 2007, which formed the policy context for the empirical data collection reported in this book. White Papers are documents produced by the government to set out details of future policy. As an opportunity for the government to gauge opinion before presenting a Bill to Parliament, they are not binding, but are distinguishable from Green Papers, which are more explicitly consultative (UK Parliament, 2011). This period includes the first three terms of the new (or reconvened) Scottish Parliament and three governments: two Labour/Liberal Democrat coalitions (1999–2003, 2003–2007), and the minority SNP administration (2007–2011). Within this period the Scottish NHS developed from a structure of Trusts and Health Authorities to the current unified territorial Board system, with Community Health Partnerships as smaller units charged with the bulk of public involvement activity. My selection of documents includes the major White Papers in order to analyse the content relevant to participation.

- *Our National Health – a plan for action, a plan for change* (Scottish Executive, 2000) can be understood as a hastily 'kilted' version of the Westminster Government's *NHS Plan.*
- *Partnership for Care* (Scottish Executive, 2003) was seen, by contrast, to make a significant break with UK government policy in dissolving Trusts.
- *Delivering for Health* (Scottish Executive, 2005). The Government response to Building a Health Service Fit for the Future (National Framework Advisory Group, 2005), this document focuses on issues of service redesign and the continued viability of rural hospitals.
- The SNP administration's key White Paper is *Better Health, Better Care* (The Scottish Government, 2007).

There are other policy documents which deal more specifically with public involvement (for example Scottish Executive, 2004, 2001; Scottish Health Council, 2010), but the relative emphasis on public involvement within the broader health policy agenda – competing with topics such as clinical priorities, health inequalities, efficiency targets, and service design – is instructive.

Identifying the proposals for action associated with participation helps to move beyond the appeal of 'warmly persuasive word[s]' (Williams, 1976, p. 76). While the symbolic power of rhetoric can be understood as one type of policy instrument (Schneider and Ingram, 1990), my concern here is with proposals for action. These are presented in Table 2.1, separated into proposals which relate to individual (patient) involvement and to collective (public) involvement. While not always a straightforward judgement – as will be discussed below – this is primarily a distinction between policy proposals which seek to directly improve patient experience at the individual level, and those which seek to strengthen the public's collective role as a stakeholder (Forster and Gabe, 2008).

Our National Health contains six proposals which relate to individual involvement. These include processes for patient complaints and feedback, patient information, patient advocacy, and several proposals around patient-centred services. These policy tools are characteristic of a New Labour approach to Patient and Public Involvement, focusing on increasing organisational capacity to improve individual experiences through staff training and new avenues of communication. The document also contains seven proposals which can be understood as promoting collective involvement. Two of these (guidance and training for staff responsible for public involvement; reviewing the guidance on formal consultations) bear a close resemblance to the capacity-building tools of individual involvement. Another, the announcement of a review of the Local Health Councils, replicates decisions being made in England at the same time about the future of Community Health Councils. The call for local government to have a stronger voice on Health Boards resembles later proposals in England to enable local authority Overview and Scrutiny Committees to have oversight of local NHS services. However, there are also proposals specific to the emerging Scottish model of unified territorial Boards. A proposal is included for a recruitment campaign to improve the diversity of Board members, hinting at the more public role which is to come. Newly formed Boards are to be supported to develop communications plans to 'rebuild the NHS in Scotland and reconnect it with patients and communities' (Scottish Executive, 2000, p. 32). Similarly, in this context familiar managerial proposals to make waiting times data more visible and accessible look quite different. Without the possibility of exit, this becomes a facilitating mechanism for collective, not individual involvement: to 'enable the public to see how their local NHS is performing' (Scottish Executive, 2000, p. 48).

Published three years later, *Partnership for Care* demonstrates far less emphasis on either individual or collective mechanisms of involvement. The overhaul of the complaints system and new mechanisms

Table 2.1 Individual and collective involvement proposals within Scottish health White Papers 2000–2007

Document	Individual measures	Collective measures
Our National Health 2000	• Overhaul complaints system • Staff training for patient-centred care • Telephone and online feedback • Project to assess and improve patient information • Partners in Charge: projects for patient-centred service change • Advocacy services	• Work with others to develop proposals for new public involvement structures (modernising Local Health Councils) • Strengthen the voice of local government on Boards • Recruitment campaign to increase diversity of decision-makers on Boards • Boards to produce annual account of public involvement and impact • Review guidance on formal consultations • Guidance and training on public involvement for staff • Make waiting times data more accessible • Boards to produce communications plans
Partnership For Care 2003	• New Statement of Entitlements and Responsibilities for patients • Staff training for patient focus • Patient Information Initiative	• Each Community Health Partnership to have a Public Partnership Forum • Creation of Scottish Health Council
Delivering for Health 2005	• Bill of Rights for patients	• Scottish Health Council to hold Boards to account annually for their public involvement activity
Better Health, Better Care 2007	• Creation of national Patient Experience programme • Patient experience to be incorporated into targets • Patients' Rights Bill including a Charter of Mutual Rights • Annual ownership report to be distributed to every household	• Review of scrutiny of major service changes • Introduction of elections for members of Health Boards • Strengthen Public Partnership Forums (including to engage with vulnerable and seldom heard) • Create a Participation Standard • Incorporate Participation Standard into performance measurement

of online and telephone feedback, both announced in *Our National Health*, are mentioned as ongoing. A new Patient Information Initiative is announced. The shift in language from patient-centred care to patient focus (as captured in the new construct Patient Focus Public Involvement (Scottish Executive, 2001)) requires a restatement of the training and capacity-building needs for staff to advance this agenda. A genuinely novel addition (although one familiar from the modern history of the UK NHS (Klein, 2010, p. 168)) is a Statement of Entitlements and Responsibilities, linking strongly to the customer-focus of 1990s Conservative and early New Labour health policy. This document proposes the transition from Local Health-Care Cooperatives to Community Health Partnerships, and the creation of Public Partnership Forums is tagged on as one sentence: 'This review [of LHCCs] should ensure that Community Health Partnerships maintain an effective dialogue with their local communities, which we envisage will be achieved through the development of a local Public Partnership Forum for each Community Health Partnership' (Scottish Executive, 2003, p. 35). The impression that PPFs are something of an afterthought is strengthened when, elsewhere in the document, Boards are to produce plans for public involvement which should merely 'take account of the local Public Partnership Forums which we envisage for each Community Health Partnership' (Scottish Executive, 2003). Collective involvement is also to be furthered by the creation of the Scottish Health Council within the existing organisation of NHS Quality Improvement Scotland. As with the continuing commitment to skills training and capacity building, this suggests that the enhancement of public involvement is primarily a technical organisational exercise, in which few conflicts of interest exist between organisations, staff, and local communities.

Delivering for Health was published in 2005, and, even more than the other documents, needs to be understood within the context of the time. Scotland's geography – including 20% of the population in areas described as 'remote and rural' in NHS terminology (Remote and Rural Steering Group, 2007) – renders the centralisation of services into regional centres an enduring issue. Professor David Kerr chaired a substantial review of the NHS in Scotland, including extensive consultative activity, which reported in 2005. This report restated the case for 'a more truly Scottish model of care ... a collective approach in which we generate strength from integration ... Patient choice is important, but the people of Scotland sent us a strong message that certainty carries greater weight' (National Framework Advisory

Group, 2005, p. 2). Recommendations included the concentration of specialised and complex care on fewer sites where clinically appropriate. *Delivering for Health*, the Scottish Executive's response, embraces this review and presents its resulting action plan. With a clear direction forward, collective public involvement is minimally included, with only one proposal, clarifying the Scottish Health Council's role in holding Boards to account for their public involvement activities. Patient focus is widely discussed, but the only significant proposal is the latest manifestation of a Bill of Rights for patients, following on from the Statement of Entitlements and Responsibilities suggested two years earlier. These proposals are presented as a response to extensive consultation with the public, and it is perhaps because of this (as well as the need for new arrangements to 'bed down') that less attention is given to the day-to-day operation of involvement at either individual or collective level. At times, public involvement is presented as a troublesome step in the process of reform: 'Our collective aim should be to implement the proposals in this plan by engaging with, and winning the support of the people we serve' (Scottish Executive, 2005, p. 54).

When the SNP took power as a minority government in May 2007 they quickly established both the NHS generally, and public involvement specifically, as priorities. In June 2007, Health Secretary Nicola Sturgeon reversed the decision to close two Accident and Emergency departments and announced a presumption against centralisation of health services, arguing that 'The two Boards did not in my view give sufficient weight to the concerns expressed by local people' (BBC News Online, 2007). *Better Health Better Care*, published in December 2007, uses the rhetoric of mutuality to underline a new vision for the Scottish NHS. It contains four proposals which I consider relevant to the individual level of involvement, and seven at the collective level. Individual level proposals include the by now familiar inclusion of a patients' charter, but this time to be enshrined in law and with the addition of a reference to mutuality: a Charter of Mutual Rights. A concern with patient focus manifests itself in proposals for the creation of a national Patient Experience programme, and the inclusion of patient experience data in performance management. The assertion of the public's 'co-ownership' of the NHS complicates ostensibly individualistic proposals such as an annual Ownership Report for every household in Scotland. While the name and some of the proposed content – details on how to get involved with influencing services locally – seem to sit at the collective level, more conventional information on patient rights and responsibilities, accessing services, and complaining about treatment are more akin to the individual level aims of informing and educating patients. At the collective level, the direct election of non-executive members of Health Boards is certainly the most eye-catching of the proposals. However, this aside, collective proposals are modest and consistent with existing policy. The role of Public Partnership Forums is confirmed, with a proposal to strengthen them. In a progression of the annual review of public involvement activity, the Scottish Health Council is asked to produce a unified 'Participation Standard' to be integrated into the performance measurement for Boards. Finally, in the wake of the controversy over Accident and Emergency closures, a review of the procedures for scrutiny of major service changes is announced.

Overall, the emphasis given to issues of public involvement varies across the four documents, with no clear chronological trend. *Our National Health* devotes one of nine chapters to 'involving people', and *Better Health, Better Care* shows an even greater focus, with 'Towards a mutual NHS' as one of three chapters. By contrast, *Partnership for Care* contains one chapter called 'Listening to patients' and then a sub-section 'Public involvement' within a different chapter concerned primarily with service change. This separation presents public involvement as a distinct activity, mostly relevant in the case of contentious service changes. The contents page for *Delivering for Health* mentions neither public involvement nor patient focus. Particularly in the case of collective mechanisms of involvement *Our National Health*, the earliest document, and *Better Health, Better Care*, the latest document, display considerably more attention than the intervening two papers, despite coming from different political parties. Accordingly, there appear to be peaks in interest in public involvement in the first White Paper after devolution and the first White Paper of the new SNP administration, with something of a lull in the intervening years. This gap is interesting, as debates on health policy in this period were preoccupied with controversy over hospital closures and the future configuration of services. That public involvement was not seen as integral to these debates suggests that it was seen as a realm of activity removed from high-level decision-making. Despite the stronger emphasis on public involvement in *Our National Health* (indicating that enthusiasm for the issue crosses party boundaries) I argue that a distinctive understanding of public involvement emerges most clearly in the SNP's *Better Health, Better Care*.

This is an analysis of proposal, not action. Some proposals are never implemented, and at other times legislation passes without prior inclusion in White Papers. One example of this is the statutory duty for

Boards to involve the public, contained in the National Health Service Reform (Scotland) Act 2003, but not included in *Partnership for Care*. As a minority government until May 2011, SNP proposals have been particularly subject to delays and change. In their first term they struggled to move forward with much of their agenda, and relatively few of these proposals have come to fruition. Others have been subject to significant delays and/or amendments. The commitment to directly elected Health Boards was reduced to a pilot scheme in the face of opposition. The Charter of Mutual Rights has become a Charter of Patient Rights and Responsibilities, contained within a Patients' Rights Act passed in February 2011. The Ownership Report has, like several Patients' Charters in the past (Forster and Gabe, 2008), become essentially a guide to accessing services. While a new 'Participation Standard' has been developed (Scottish Health Council, 2010) it is yet to be integrated into the national system of performance management. Proposals to strengthen Public Partnership Forums have not materialised. While they remain in place their role has shifted subtly from being 'the main way' (Scottish Executive, 2004, p. 4) in which the NHS involves the public to being one of 'many different ways' of 'listening and responding' (Scottish Health Council, 2010, p. 16). At least from a structural perspective, on-the-ground public involvement does not appear transformed, particularly in Boards which are not piloting elections. However, *Better Health, Better Care* remains interesting not in terms of its success in translating a vision into reality, but in terms of the extent to which it demonstrates an alternative vision of public involvement.

While staying firmly within the toolbox of public involvement policies described above, the distinctiveness of *Better Health, Better Care* lies in its shift from interest in collective mechanisms of advice (such as Public Partnership Forums) to those of control (such as directly elected Board members). Despite the pervasive and eye-catching rhetoric of mutuality, *Better Health, Better Care* turns instead to more traditional tools of control of health organisations. The introduction of direct elections to Health Boards is the most self-evidently oppositional tactic, but the proposal to incorporate assessments of public involvement into performance management systems is similarly aggressive. In a sense, the ungainly, peculiarly Scottish descriptor 'Patient Focus Public Involvement' only really begins to have meaning in 2007, as the day-to-day business of engaging with current patients is firmly separated from the questions of collective control which preoccupy *Better Health, Better Care*. I do not claim in this evolution a 'better' or 'worse' (or 'weaker' or 'stronger') conception of public involvement. Turning away from the temptation to evaluate public involvement along linear hierarchies, I would argue that the SNP's interpretation of public involvement locates proposals primarily at the level of organisational governance, while a New Labour interpretation offers an advisory function which is integrated more extensively with the (privatised) patient realm than the (public, even political) realm of the citizen.

While a shift in emphasis and rhetoric is evident, these are not path-breaking reforms. The recurrence of a charter of patient rights is familiar. Terminology stays consistent and structures of involvement for members of the public to oversee organisations are left broadly unchanged, with Public Partnership Forums and the Scottish Health Council subject to reviews but left intact (FMR Research, 2008; Scottish Councils Foundation and McCormick-McDowell, 2008; Scottish Health Council, 2009). The invocation of mutuality, often used as shorthand for the whole SNP health policy agenda, is something of a rhetorical red herring. Mutuality in the public sector and in healthcare has a long pedigree (Birchall, 2001; Gorsky et al., 2005), but is more often associated with non-universal, exclusive organisations. As Birchall (2008, p. 5) argues, mutualism 'has sometimes been used as a vague call to involve citizens more closely in decision made over public services. However, properly used it refers to a membership-based organisation, in which the users of services are in control of provision'. The compatibility of a genuinely mutual organisation with the Scottish policy commitment to universality is questionable. In experimenting with membership models for the elections for Boards of Governors, English Foundation Trusts found that opt-out (i.e. universal) membership was an expensive exercise which yielded dramatically low election turnout (Day and Klein, 2005). The SNP's proposals are overtly inclusive; indeed, they seek to bring all the 'people of Scotland' into a closer relationship with the NHS. Despite the strong rhetoric of mutuality, many of the policy tools for public involvement proposed in *Better Health, Better Care* actually draw on a far more traditional hierarchical approach.

While distinguishing the individual from the collective dimensions of involvement is a useful starting point, this analysis demonstrates the limits of the approach. Instead of a switch in Scottish health policy from instruments of individual involvement to those of collective involvement, there are nuanced differences in approach and emphasis. There are behavioural assumptions at play in the selection of policy tools. Schneider and Ingram (1990) suggest that capacity-building tools (for example the provision of training, support, and information to both staff and patients) assume that the policy goals are shared and welcome, and that obstacles are of ability, not willingness. By contrast, *Better Health, Better Care* primarily relies upon authority tools (mandating of elections), incentive tools (incorporation of patient experience and public involvement measures into performance management), and symbolic tools (the rhetoric of mutuality and co-ownership), suggesting that their diagnosis of problems is of organisational intransigence, not inability. This is in keeping with some of the more inflammatory statements of SNP Health Secretary Nicola Sturgeon: 'Elected health boards ... are the best way of ensuring that boards will no longer be able to ride roughshod over community opinion, as has happened in the past' (The Scottish Government, 2009). Context is also crucial. The distinctiveness of the current Scottish approach is in part due to the structural consequences of other reforms. In a unified territorial system – where planning and not commissioning is the primary task – there is far more scope to have input from a collective manifestation of the local population. It is no coincidence that electing members of health authorities was a recurring proposal in health policy debates up until the late 1990s (Hunter and Harrison, 1997; Klein and Lewis, 1976; Klein and New, 1998): Scotland's traditional NHS structure lends itself to traditional policy tools. In this context, the dividing line between individual and collective involvement is blurred. As with the publication of waiting times data, *Better Together*, the programme for the collection of data on patient experience appears intrinsically individual. However, it is widely publicised in order to aid the public in holding local services to account. This, then, is a tool of individual involvement put to collective purposes.

Careful attention to policy documents reveals a significant evolution in approach since devolution in Scotland. Where the early introduction of the construct 'Patient Focus Public Involvement' can be seen as a path-breaking commitment to a more collective approach, the proposals associated were far more consistent with the prior model of involvement. Thus while the broader organisational structures of the Scottish NHS began to diverge significantly from the pre-devolution model (and from those elsewhere in the UK) from 2003, the overall approach to the public's role in the management of services was reasonably consistent until the introduction of the SNP's *Better Health, Better Care* in 2007. Beneath ostensibly consistent terminology and, to a lesser extent, structures, this document reignites debates about the accountability of NHS services to local communities which have been largely dormant since New Labour placed a more privatised interpretation of public involvement at the heart of their vision for the NHS.

Scotland among other health systems

Underneath the eye-catching banner of 'mutualism', the policy frame-work for participation in healthcare which developed in Scotland in the late 2000s and early 2010s is a mixed bag of measures with a range of influences. This eclecticism is consistent with this policy area generally: Klein's (2004, p. 207) description of 'a layer cake of initiatives, with no necessary logical link between the component parts' is relevant beyond its specific target (New Labour public involvement policy in England). Policy on citizen participation encompasses a multitude of goals, some of which may be in direct conflict with each other (Bochel et al., 2008). What makes the Scottish healthcare system in this period a particularly interesting example is the coexistence of a diverse range of what I call 'modes' of participation. This diversity reflects the 'window of oppor-tunity' described above, where devolution generated new political space, and empowered political actors, the SNP and the Scottish Liberal Democrats, more used to critiquing from the sidelines. Therefore, measures which were dormant in the figurative policy toolbox could now be experimented with alongside more familiar, tried-and-tested policies.

A central goal of this book is to adopt a wider analytic lens than that with which participation in healthcare is usually approached. Acknowledging the mix of policy tools with which central govern-ment has sought to accomplish participation in healthcare, this book takes an alternative starting point; a 'citizen's-eye' view of the Scottish health system. I describe and analyse five modes of system–public interaction in the Scottish context – committee work, outreach, repre-sentative democracy, protest, and subversive service use – which, while distinctively of their time and place in their details, hold much broader relevance internationally. Public roles on committee-style structures are widely recognisable in health systems in both high- and low-income countries, and can be understood as the default option for health sys-tems seeking to 'do' participation. Outreach work, perhaps the most diverse of my categories, encompasses most of the other short-term consultative activities which healthcare organisations customarily undertake. The shape of formal links between representative democracy and healthcare organisations are a recurring issue in all publicly funded health systems, and the specific example of directly elected boards for healthcare organisations has been tried in Canada, New Zealand, and England, as well as Scotland (Stewart et al., 2015). Public protest and campaigns targeting unpopular decisions of healthcare organisations have been widely studied, with literature on anti-hospital closure campaigns prevalent in Canada, the USA, and Scandinavia, as well as the UK. Finally, my 'wild card' category of subversive tactics of service use, while not conventionally understood as a facet of public participation, takes on features of the patient–professional relationship which will be familiar in any health system. Beyond the specific empirics of the five modes of action discussed in this book, my goal is analytic, rather than descriptive. The contextual specificities of the Scottish healthcare system will be highlighted where relevant, but the broader goals, of exploring 'invited' efforts at participation and arguing for a fuller appreciation of 'uninvited' public action, transcend the particular system from which my data are drawn.

3
Administering the System: Citizen Participation as Committee Work

Inviting citizens to join either existing or standalone committees is a key tool for healthcare organisations seeking to engage with their publics. This mode of participation is one of the most traditional ways for healthcare organisations to 'do' participation. In a systematic review of patient and public involvement in the UK NHS, Mockford et al. (2012, p. 30) identified committee-type roles ranging from 'lay membership of NHS managerial boards ... to patient involvement in condition-specific groups of individuals with a solitary aim'. In an international review, Mitton et al. (2009) include a 'standing citizens' advisory panel' as one of 15 'methods of engagement' identified, and found research reporting 51 instances of this form between 1981 and 2006. From Community Health Councils, to Public and Patient Involvement Forums, to Local Involvement Networks and Local Healthwatch, the UK, and latterly English, NHS has repeatedly turned to the creation of standing committee-style spaces as the key route for public influence in local healthcare organisations (Baggott, 2005; Mullen et al., 2011). The Australian health system has 'Community Advisory Committees' with similar remits (Mack, 2010). Lay representatives can be chosen either to represent a generic 'lay' perspective, or to compensate for the under-representation of specific groups. In New Zealand, District Health Boards are mandated to have two representatives of the Maori population (Boulton et al., 2004). In this chapter I consider any ongoing public representation within an 'invited space' created by healthcare organisations as examples of 'committee work', regardless of the varied terminology of councils, forums, and groups.

Citizen participation as committee work has three key characteristics. Firstly, the citizens who populate these committees have no formal link back to the wider public. While some might make their way onto the committees by virtue of their particular experience within, for example, voluntary or community organisations, their claims to representation (where articulated) are informal. Secondly, this type of work is primarily bureaucratic, and depends upon citizens adopting the standard operating procedures of the modern, managerial healthcare organisation. Finally, and relatedly, this is the sort of ongoing involvement (over a period of weeks, if not years) that asks more from citizens than a one-off survey completion or meeting attendance. In this chapter I will discuss each of these defining characteristics in turn, before exploring two manifestations of public committee work in the contemporary NHS in Scotland.

The lack of formal 'authorisation' of public representatives in committee work is a widely recognised issue, and yet it is a criticism which is rarely convincingly articulated. The spectre of 'the usual suspects' has haunted the policy and practice of public involvement mechanisms in the UK. As far back as 1975, Community Health Councils were criticised by NHS staff for being 'unrepresentative' (Ham, 1980), and this complaint was also directed at their successor organisations, Public and Patient Involvement Forums (House of Commons – Health Committee, 2007). Academic literature on public involvement has largely failed to offer a convincing response to these criticisms: Crawford et al. (2003, p. 46) find 'statements about representativeness are very common in the literature, but the meaning of the term is rarely considered'. Learmonth et al. (2009) discuss the 'Catch 22' of populating involvement mechanisms with individuals who are simultaneously seen as 'ordinary', but who also have the time, confidence, and skill set to be, as policy demands, 'effective' on committees.

The second characteristic of committee work is that it brings members of the public into the bureaucratic heart of healthcare governance. Freeman (2008) identifies committees as a specific type of meeting where the roles are formal and the rules are explicit.

> 'not much is made of meetings in the public policy and related literature. Seemingly mundane and certainly more "micro" than many other disciplinary concerns, they appear to have been "black-boxed"'. (Freeman, 2008, p. 4)

Committees remain a crucial part of decision-making (and decision-sanctioning) in most, if not all, health systems. While the public administration literature is replete with claims that public organisations have moved from hierarchical structures towards markets or networks

(Rhodes, 1997), other have pointed to the continued co-existence of organisational forms (Exworthy et al., 1999). While committees are perhaps most associated with command-and-control hierarchies, they are as likely to be present in quasi-market and network-based health systems. Accordingly, how and what committees do (and are perceived to do within organisations) remains relevant. Being part of a committee entails a number of roles and responsibilities, often formalised into agreed 'rules' (such as 'standing orders' or 'terms of reference'). While simple membership is a role in itself (and in some cases having a nominated 'lay' person listed within a committee's membership may do enough to demonstrate 'public involvement'), there is generally an expectation of attendance at meetings (whether 'real' or 'virtual'). In identifying committees as a key *modus operandi* of contemporary health systems, I do not intend to suggest that they invariably wield significant power. Indeed, the example of specially created 'advisory' committees with little or no decision-making power is likely to demonstrate quite the opposite. Rather, committees (their existence and their meetings) can be understood as the skeleton of an organisational chart of most health systems. Accordingly, this chapter explores the way that citizen participation occurs within and around this skeleton of committees, including the roles that public participants play within decision-making processes therein.

The final characteristic of public committee work as a mode of participation is that it is an ongoing responsibility, in contrast to the one-off, bounded engagements described in Chapter 4's 'outreach' projects. As Harrison and Mort (1998, p. 62) put it, this gives the opportunity for members of the public to develop 'a representative role or identity, rather than as a one-off *ad hoc* phenomenon'. While some of the outreach projects described in Chapter 4 lasted as long as the tenure of some public members of the committees described in this chapter, the difference is the expectation of prolonged engagement and a future-oriented contribution to the decision-making process. Thus members of the public involved in committee work are likely to be expected to learn and develop expertise in the subject matter of the committee, as opposed to participants in an outreach-type snapshot which seeks to obtain an 'account of public opinion as it "really" is' (Harrison and Mort, 1998, p. 64).

Public work on committees in the Scottish NHS

This chapter explores data from observation and interviews with citizens involved in two distinct but similar types of public NHS committees. Firstly, I present data on individuals who are invited to sit on existing Health Board committees (for example Clinical Governance or

Audit) alongside senior staff members, Executive and Non-Executive Directors. Secondly, I present findings from a Public Partnership Forum, a standalone committee composed only of members of the public, which fed into Board decision-making. PPFs have been required for every local area in the Scottish NHS since 2003. In this time their role has shifted from being 'the main way' (Scottish Executive, 2004, p. 4) the NHS involves the public to being one of 'many different ways' of 'listening and responding' (Scottish Health Council, 2010, p. 16).

Lay representatives on Board committees

Lay representatives on Board committees are non-remunerated positions in which citizens are expected to give a non-specialist perspective on NHS decisions. In this they are, as Hogg and Williamson (2001, p. 3) note, 'defined, not by the positive attributes that they might have, but by who they are not and what they do not have'. In the territorial Health Boards where data was collected, Board committees all had at least one lay member who attended meetings, and most had several. The lines between lay representatives and the remunerated non-executive Board members (as discussed further in Chapter 5) who are also appointed to sit on committees are more blurred in theory than in practice. NHS Boards and their committees are populated by significant numbers of citizens acting as non-executive directors, and working alongside a smaller number of 'lay representatives'. However, in interviews and observation, there was little suggestion of overlap between the two types of role. In the Board from which interview data is drawn, efforts to recruit more widely to Board membership were taking place, but few interviewees reported seeing lay membership as a route to Board membership.

This Board had recently increased the number of lay representatives on its committees, advertising in the local press for volunteers and undertaking a relatively formal recruitment process. One of the six lay representatives I interviewed had come across the opportunity in this way ('I was reading a paper on something or other and at the bottom of the paper there was a, you know, NHS are looking for volunteers and a link, you know. So I went to the link and I applied'), but all others had heard about the opportunities through word of mouth. All described being well-connected within their communities and/or the local voluntary sector. As with PPF members discussed below, one committee role often led on to others:

Ann: I've been a lay representative for 14 years so and what you tend to find is if you get onto one committee suddenly you're in demand because they're always very short of lay representatives so you get onto other committees.

Representatives were all retired (in some cases early) and when describing their reasons for volunteering on committees, gave a mixture of three linked reasons. Firstly, many were grateful to and committed to the NHS, expressing 'a desire to try and put something back in, you know, to the service I'd had so much from'. Secondly, most felt they had some knowledge, often gleaned from personal experience of service use, or in a few cases, professional skills from their working life, which could be helpful. This in some cases stemmed from mild dissatisfaction with services, not sufficient to complain, but merely to seek some change.

Maureen: Whilst the care was excellent there were just certain things that I felt I could have input in, into making a better service.

Ann: I'd had like years' experience of attending the hospital on a regular basis as well as obviously having contact with your GP and everything and you know I could see loads of areas where they could ... just a very slight improvement could improve the system ... but you had no means or any way of actually saying to somebody, you know, 'why don't you do ... ?'

Finally, and most commonly, representatives described being keen to 'do something' in retirement to keep busy and active:

Maureen: I felt it would benefit me in that I didn't want my brain to stagnate after working for so long

Agnes: Because I retired when I was relatively young, it was like 'well, what am I going to do, this is not going to be the rest of my life'?

Interviewees ranged from those involved with NHS committees for over a decade to those appointed in the previous few months. Newer members referred to a learning curve, and in some cases to feeling slightly intimidated by the context:

Alexander: As far as contribution is concerned it's difficult at the moment, there's a lot of people, you know it's a big committee and I have no specific expertise in any of the areas that they're talking about to any great extent

Several newer members said that as yet, they spoke rarely. However, others criticised lay members who took a more cautious approach.

Ann: I think the other thing is that you've got to sort of show that you're not intimidated if you like by the various Board members that are going to be sitting, you know, there's no point in going on a committee unless you're willing to speak up. Whereas I have been on committees where you have lay representatives who never open their mouth if you know what I mean. Now even if you're actually not ... to me it's like even if you're not exactly making a fool of yourself but you know if there's something you don't understand there's no point in continuing along and then still not understanding it, you're better sort of saying 'can you just explain that to me?' or go for it.

The most common understanding of the lay representative role was one of scrutiny. This involved doing substantial quantities of reading and then asking 'appropriate' questions. Reading was described as onerous by all representatives interviewed:

Liz: The reading is very heavy, there are a lot of papers, but as a committee member it's my duty to make sure that I read them not just once but several times.

Alexander: Now the first committee meeting I went to I got emailed to me papers for the committee and there was well over 500 pages of reading. I had a week to read them and absorb them.

Asking questions was, for most members, central to the role. However, most expressed concern about ensuring that their questions were appropriate to the setting:

Maureen: To ask pertinent questions when they're relevant, I don't see my role as just to speak, because I'm there, which I think is daft but, and I feel from an outsider's point of view if I think they're pertinent things to say.

There was more variation in how representatives described the basis from which they asked questions. Several described using their technical skills to bring new perspectives to committees.

Ann: Before I retired basically my job it was looking at how to improve things and looking at ways to be more efficient. So I brought that to, you know, all the different groups that I've sat on.

Alexander: At the last meeting I was at ... somebody had put together a report and I thought [it] was pretty poor and I kind of said as much. I didn't say it was poor, I just tried to point out that there were better ways of doing it.

In both these cases, representatives with significant technical expertise from their professional careers described being proud to apply them to the business of the committees they sat on, albeit with a cautious attitude when new to the committee ('the last thing I want to do is get off on the wrong foot with people by saying their service is crap').

The appropriateness, or not, of bringing one's personal experiences to the formal bureaucratic context of the committee was more contested. For the majority of my interviewees, knowledge gained through experience as a patient was out of place in what everyone described as a very formal setting.

Alexander: I don't see any particular place for me to say, you know, 'well when I was in the [hospital] such and such ...', you know, I don't think that is a part and parcel of it.

However, several interviewees, even where they did not see *their own* personal experience as appropriate to share in the committee setting, acknowledged a useful role for this information from other lay representatives:

Alexander: You know, the fact that [another lay representative] comes out with the stuff she comes out with about, you know, the [number 7] bus and that sort of stuff, it brings a level of reality into the thing that maybe isn't there.

That 'reality' was also important to one lay member who stressed her knowledge of public perspectives as the justification for both her presence and her specific contributions in meetings:

Liz: I'm involved in various other committees not just [here] but nationally as well. It works out fine because I hear things and go to different meetings and, you know, various places where you hear things and people tell you [things], you know.

In sum, these lay representatives, who had been invited to sit on NHS committees, found themselves negotiating a highly formalised bureaucratic context with a somewhat ambiguous role. The workload, especially the reading, was onerous, and the environment could be intimidatingly formal and technical. The nature of the contribution expected of these lay representatives – whether technical or an outside 'lay' perspective – was for individuals to work out *in situ*. For all, however, the desire to contribute stemmed from commitment to the mission of the NHS and a desire for a purposive role in retirement.

Public Partnership Forums

Public Partnership Forums (PPFs) are another example of public 'committee work' in the Scottish NHS. Although a statutory requirement across Scotland, the form that PPFs take is not prescribed by central government. The PPF I studied in Rivermouth involved individuals (mostly recruited from existing community groups) meeting regularly to respond to developments and requests from the local NHS. There was also a larger mailing list of interested citizens, who were occasionally asked to comment on new developments. The limited empirical literature on PPFs (FMR Research, 2008) indicates that this Forum is fairly conventional in its approach and structures.

Within Rivermouth, the PPF was but one of many actors working on public involvement. This could be a resource, but could also prompt confusion and competition between different groups. With its statutory legitimacy, some understood the PPF to be the main avenue of participation; others saw it as merely one among many. This resonates with accounts of the demise of Community Health Councils in England, where they became one among many bodies claiming to represent the public (Pickard, 1997). The PPF was the obvious anchor for public involvement within the CHP (having no other purpose for existence), but few interviewees in the wider CHP, were very familiar with its role.

In terms of its day-to-day operation, Rivermouth PPF was an odd hybrid of two different types of organisation. With loose, ill-defined criteria for membership, attempts at creation of an online network of participants, and occasionally nebulous feel it resembled a governance network: 'a web of relationships between government … and civil society actors … dispersed, flexible and in some cases transparent modes of agenda-setting, policy-making and implementation' (Klijn and Skelcher, 2007). However, in meetings it functioned like a traditional bureaucratic committee with a pre-defined agenda including 'standing' items, all debate channelled through the Chair, and discussion neatly minuted. This hybrid approach can be understood as a result of the statutory mandate for the existence of a PPF: because the Forum had been mandated to exist before anyone had a clear sense of what it should be or do, it had evolved peculiarly, with a great sense of urgency that things should be seen to happen and yet an overwhelming lack of consensus on why. Members' memories of the (abolished) Local Health Council, as well as similar spaces outwith the health system, shaped emerging practice. As Davies et al. (2006, p. 200) eloquently describe in the case of the NICE Citizens Council: 'although [it] had zero history in itself, the mix of discursive practices which came to constitute it trail behind them convoluted histories'.

The PPF was four years old at the time of my fieldwork, and most of its members had been directly recruited by the CHP, by sending letters to known voluntary health and social care groups in the area, or by approaching former members of the disbanded Local Health Council. Other members had heard about the PPF from friends. Several were experienced committee members, who had often 'graduated' from a local major Board-wide consultation exercise a decade earlier. James had a particularly convoluted route on to the PPF, including personal invitations. He was, in many ways, the archetypal 'usual suspect'.

James: I ended up as Chair of the Health Council ... And then Scottish Health Council took all the local ones over, eh, so I was sort of kicking around for about six months or so and then the Chair of the Health Board then phoned me up and said would you be interested in coming round to the Community Health Partnership when it was first formed? So I said yes, and I didn't realise in what capacity I was going on for the time being because the PPF hadn't been formed then. But eventually I was public representative on the CHP – that was my role. Then the CHP came along, the PPF came along and, eh, I became a member of that.

Often members could not quite remember at which point they had heard about or joined the PPF; they were well connected in their community and it could have been from a number of different contacts or mailing lists.

Michael: it's one of these things that sort of creeps up on you in a sense, cause I was in, I joined the, em, heart support group side of the CHP. And I think the option to become involved in this came through that ..., em, since, but it was through that I think just a sort of widening membership of other committees and things.

This widening membership in a range of health-related participatory activities, some overlapping between support for other patients and influencing services, is fairly characteristic of most of the PPF members.

For two members, progression into the voluntary activity which brought them to the PPF was rooted in their social worlds. Mary described the process by which she had fallen into first helping out, then coordinating, a small, informal club for people recovering from strokes.

Mary: I just said to [my friend] well look, you say to the powers that be there and just, I'll, if you ca'ae get anybody else I'll come along and dae it.

After taking over Mary began receiving *'the bumph'* (letters and information) from the Community Health Partnership, including repeated letters asking for volunteers for the PPF.

Mary: I kept getting this one aboot, for the CHP, and I says oh I'm fed up o' this, it was like every week, what are youse going to dae aboot it? 'Oh you just answer it Mary and eh, we'll see'. I says right. So I got an answer back they were wanting tae interview me aboot going on the committee. Now I'm no' a committee person. Right? ... So that's how I then got up on the committee.

Interviewer: And what, what do you mean you're not a committee person? What sort of thing?

Mary: Well, the thing is, well the ... [the previous organiser of the club] decided what they done and when they done it, but since she's died, they have to decide, and then I make it work. And that's, me. There's nae point sitting' blethering if you're nae going tae do the job. With anything like that.

Mary had fallen into participation through very informal volunteering in her community, and described initial feelings of irritation and suspicion at requests for her to enter the world of 'committee people'. Margaret, more straightforwardly, had heard about the PPF from a friend and enquired directly. Both described their entry into the PPF as located within social networks.

As 'new' entrants to the world of committees, Mary and Margaret were not 'usual suspects' like James or William, but by a peculiar logic their membership of the PPF transformed them instantly into usual suspects. The fear is that a small group of 'elite' participants – or 'expert citizens' (Bang, 2005) – are over-represented on many committees within the governance of a local area (as Mary put it 'a' these men seem tae dae nothing but go to this committee, that committee, and the next committee'.) Behind this fear lie underspecified parallels with more traditional political activity; PPF membership as the equivalent of giving a small, particular group of the population multiple opportunities to vote in an election. However, this underestimates the extent to which participation within the PPF was conducted with a strong focus on 'the public good' and a suspicious attitude towards actors seen as pursuing self or group interest.

As an example of invited public participation, those setting up the PPF appeared to have made a genuine attempt to create space for members to define its mode of operation. Beyond the PPF 'manual' – a document couched in the most vague and general of terms – there was no 'official' statement of appropriate PPF membership. No formal training was given to new members, and there was no evidence in either observation or interviews of more subtle forms of censure from staff. If anything, the opposite is true; new members wanted more direction, and in interviews, several quizzed me as to what the PPF should be doing. One of the newest members repeatedly asked me about her role:

Margaret: But I'm just not sure that we're absolutely clear in relation to what sort of clout we have! If any! You know? I mean can we go along there and say 'no, this is not on'?

This member's concerns around the PPF's 'clout' (i.e. influence) points at the way in which existing modes of behaviour in the PPF shaped understandings of appropriate behaviour, but also demonstrates the way in which new members confronted ambiguity about the nature and purposes of membership. In the absence of instructions, the Forum, many of whom were founder members, had chosen to develop a very conventional system of monthly formal meetings with an agenda and minutes. Spending a year observing these decorous meetings in formal conference rooms, and talking to members of the Forum in coffee breaks and car parks, I was surprised at the lack of challenge or contest in the day-to-day life of the PPF. Rather than being a locus of demands for power, the PPF as an institution was largely a site for work and a sense of personal usefulness.

In an attempt to make sense of this, I constructed three ideal-type 'styles' of Forum membership to explore both role and type of activity in participants' own understandings of why they are part of the Forum and what they are there to do. These styles emerged directly from discussions with Forum members (and in the case of the volunteer/consultant distinction, from a heated debate observed in a Forum meeting). They describe ways of being a PPF member, and not types of people. In this PPF it seemed clear that (behavioural) roles were available between which members could, within the inevitable constraints of the social context, shift. Some PPF members mostly seemed to operate within a particular style, but most shifted about, and some seemed 'stuck' operating in a style which did not correspond with the motivations they described in interviews.

Most of the members I spoke to simply joined the Forum in order to be 'helpful': their motivation was more akin to that of a traditional volunteer than interest representation.

James: It's going back to the original idea of joining the NHS as a volunteer ... I thought ... I'd like to do something to sort of show that I'm not completely just sitting back and just getting benefits.

Members also emphasised that they enjoyed the opportunity to learn more about the NHS locally. Members had been recruited to the PPF through existing volunteer work in health-related community groups, and the Forum was for many of them an extension of this work. One member had a long history of trade union and political party activism, as well as voluntary caring work. When I asked her whether she enjoyed the role she replied:

Mary: Enjoying it is not the word. It's something that people need to do. That's how I see it. They wouldn't come in and send me the letters to come and interview me, to put me on the committee, if there wasn't somewhere along the line I was going to be able to, thought I maybe could give something.

This member saw Forum membership as part of her duty in the community (to give an as yet unspecified 'something'), rather than as part of her (political) activism to change things.

Most members had few preconceived ideas about what the PPF *should* be doing, preferring to await requests for assistance:

Donald: We often have people in giving talks ... and they ask us for comments ... And we'll give our comments, and they usually take them on board and they'll come back another time and say how they've got on. Eh, and how the comments that we've made have made a difference or not.

This member's description suggests equanimity on the question of influence. Making a difference, or not, is something of an afterthought, and the priority is simply to respond to a request for help.

The nature of the help was often about making up numbers at the meetings, doing the reading, or putting one's hand up at the appropriate moment to nominate or second the minutes. For some members, simply attending everything they were invited to could add up to a significant amount of work (in one of the Chair's reports he had represented the Forum at nine events in the previous month, as well as preparing for the regular meeting). While members all told me that they would speak up if unhappy about a development, this situation rarely arose. When requests came to the PPF, for example when volunteers were sought to run a stall in the hospital foyer promoting hand hygiene, this was a welcome example of 'actually getting to do something':

Margaret: You know ... going along for example to the hand hygiene, I felt that had some influence on people, coming in to visit or use the service and things like that, because you could actually demonstrate to them, look this is what we need you to do, here's the reason why, here's how you do it properly.

The welcome potential for influence here was influencing the public at large, not the organisation. It therefore cohered neatly with a 'service' orientation ('directly helping those in need' (Harre, 2007)) and was most prevalent where members identified uncontroversial, straightforward needs. Echoing Roberts and Devine's (2004) finding that participants often reject the label of activist, members often seemed to find this a more comfortable or appropriate role than one which sought to challenge or change the NHS.

Several members described an alternative, more project-based 'consultancy' role for the Forum, where issues would be explored in depth rather than being discussed briefly at one meeting. One member envisioned a role for the Forum akin to that of a market research consultancy, planning and carrying out small pieces of research on public opinion.

Thomas: It's almost like if you were in a private company you wanted to do some advertising, you want to get your message across, and so you employ a marketing agent or a whatever, a PR type organisation, and, say right this is the message I want to give.

The PPF here is envisaged as a conduit, with members offering communication skills and not their opinions.

Another member explicitly used the language of consultancy when discussing his role in the Forum. He performed skilled tasks for the CHP and the Board, such as reviewing building plans for appropriate disability access, and was irritated when a member of staff came along to one meeting to talk about the Board's Investing in Volunteers award. The member of staff began her presentation with 'You probably don't see yourself as volunteers, but the public involvement you are doing is volunteering'. In our subsequent interview, one member disputed this.

Thomas: We're not volunteers ... All volunteers with the NHS have sort of managers, and people who organise them and whatnot. Nobody organises me. Nobody tells me what to do, where to go, when to be there for. We're totally different.

This member distinguished himself from 'the volunteers' on the basis of his specific knowledge and expertise, his role within an external group, and his autonomy and independence.

The external image of the Forum (as suggested by staff members interviewed, and by visitors to Forum meetings) seemed to be that of a group of experts on consulting the public.

James: a sounding board, so that when people were actually passing information out to the public ... they'd run it past us, the methodology that would do it.

Being in this 'expert' position carried risk for members who had no particular expertise in such methods. When 'minor' service changes were proposed it was unclear whether the PPF should be a first port of call for staff members to help advise on the consultation, or should be part of the consultation. For a consultation on a service change proposal, Forum members had suggested a series of public meetings, which had then been very poorly attended.

Thomas: It wasn't dealt with in a detailed way, it was dealt with at a meeting, a presentation, 'What would you think?' Well, you could have meetings in certain areas around. A good suggestion, for what it was worth, didn't work out at all. They got nobody to the meetings so we had to come back and revisit.

This anecdote demonstrates the risks of consultancy, as opposed to the volunteering image of purveyors of common-sense or a patient's-eye view. Being seen as an expert entails a sense of responsibility when things go wrong.

There was little in this Forum that seemed challenging to the local NHS organisation, and members almost never spoke in such adversarial terms. I include this style almost for its absence, and because expectations of it (as described in extant literature) shaped the research. Indeed, in some cases members put aside issues that they felt strongly about in order to adopt a 'helping' orientation within the Forum. One campaigned for disabled groups in his spare time, but was adamant (and observation and analysis of the minutes support this) that he would not raise such issues through the Forum.

James: I keep politics out of it. You know I would say that's my fight that I'm fighting, that's nothing to do with the, the PPF, so that's never brought up.

In Forum meetings occasional moments of challenge rarely made it out of the realm of 'banter' round the table. In one discussion of the delay in renovating a local building, a member asked why the Chief Executive of the Board was getting a pay rise when this project was held up by a lack of funds. The comment was laughed off good-humouredly, and when I asked him about it later he shrugged and smiled.

The closest this Forum had to a challenging member had joined the Forum through his activism in the local disability group, and his specific interests did shape his activities.

Thomas: There have been, in the past wee while, a couple of things that I would have liked to branched out from there and got involved in. But to be honest, I don't have the time, you know.

And they weren't, em, [my area of interest] wasn't really involved an awful lot in these particular things.

Present on his own terms and with his own goals in mind, this member was distinguished from the rest of the group by his autonomy, and he could also be relied upon to proactively ask difficult questions on the basis of his particular interests.

I understand these differences in the practice of PPF membership as tensions within the local assemblage of public involvement. Li (2007) outlines six key practices which maintain assemblages, including 'managing failures and contradictions'. These are managed, rather than resolved, through 'fuzziness, adjustment and compromise' (Li, 2007, p. 279). A good example of this was the revision of terms of reference for the PPF during my fieldwork. This involved the document being posted out to all members, and an item placed on the agenda where members could raise changes they wanted to make. The catalyst for the discussion was the Chair's suggestion that the terms be amended to reflect the fact that the PPF would comment on the substance, as well as the methodology, of consultations brought before them. This distinction was an important one in practice, as for example when a manager brought a proposal for a two-day consultation event on the proposed closure of a ward (with the service being moved into the community). The existing patients and their carers had already been consulted and were apparently satisfied. In this situation the group were consulted as experts on public involvement, and asked for their views on the 'methodology' of the consultation. However, the requirement for an instant response meant there was little they could contribute beyond broadly supporting the idea of a consultation event.

Analytically, this change to the PPF's constitution involved official acknowledgement of the lay volunteer and, potentially, the challenging roles that some PPF members preferred to play, instead of the official 'expert' consultant role. However, there was no ranking of roles, or editing of the existing understanding of the PPF. More roles were added, but none were taken away; the PPF's uncertain purpose was simply made 'fuzzier'. The discussion was not merely about debating the PPF as an 'out-there' entity, but actually creating it (Barnes, 1993), with the words on paper ('terms of reference') as tangible evidence of its existence. As an observer, this discussion seemed to be avoiding the central question of purpose. Jennifer, the NHS staff member minuting the meeting, tried to outline her vision of a public involvement role which Litva et al. (2009) describe as 'overseeing', entreating members to 'be like the police' in committees, watching out for problems from a patient's-eye view. This role divides between two of my ideal-type PPF members, requiring both the regular, dogged presence of volunteers and the willingness to hold to account of a 'challenging' style. It was the closest anyone came during my fieldwork to attempting to state an 'official' role for the PPF.

The previous section describes three different potential membership styles to demonstrate the considerable distance between members' understandings of their roles within the PPF. Although overt disagreement very rarely surfaced in meetings, in interviews it became clear that members were aware that the PPF was not a unified group with the same understanding of their purpose. Given the unclear definitions of participation within the literature and policy (Martin, 2008a), uncertainties in the everyday practice of public involvement are to be expected. However, the overwhelming lack of challenging understandings of the PPF's role suggests that participation in this case study was heavily biased towards a conservative, volunteeristic frame. While this coheres with the supportive role that policy sets out for PPFs (Scottish Executive, 2004), it is more problematic for a political, 'Arnsteinian' understanding of contemporary participation.

As discussed in Chapter 1, typologies of participation still tend to assess how much power or influence a mechanism gives to the public. The power available through the PPF varied, but a key finding of this research was that this was not terribly relevant to members themselves, who sought alternative roles. The volunteering style afforded a modest kind of influence. Staff who came to ask the Forum's view were respectful and attentive, and more often than not the wording of a leaflet would be changed to reflect Forum members' views. Additional tasks were welcomed, but not primarily as opportunities for agency, for Arendt's 'potentialities of action' (Arendt, 1998). These pre-defined tasks permitted minimal discretion, but fitted well with a volunteering motivation. The consultancy style affords a greater degree of influence. While still reactive, consulting brought more opportunities for change, and one member had achieved meaningful changes that would serve the interest group he represents. However, in common with the volunteering style, power was earned through work. This member worked long hours establishing himself as a recognised source of expertise, being 'at the table', and performing tasks which saved staff time or money spent hiring an external consultant. Most of the Forum members had not joined to gain power or challenge the local NHS and were content simply to perform the tasks asked of them. The essentially supportive nature of participation in the PPF confounded my expectations. From this starting point, a willingness to reactively fulfil assigned tasks makes more sense. I had expected the basic business of the Forum to have been about members expressing opinions and dissent, involving considerable discretion, but in practice they largely became about performing 'ritual' roles and giving 'expert' advice on consulting with the public. Crucially, this was the role sought by an overwhelming majority of members.

Understanding committee work as a mode of participation

These two examples of participation – a group of citizens being invited to form a standalone committee, or individual citizens being invited onto an existing organisational committee – have some key differences. PPF meetings often seemed to lack substantive content, while the lay representatives reported packed agendas, and being laden down with reading. Where the PPF came to a conclusion on an issue, this would be fed in through higher level committees, while lay representatives were physically at the committee table where decisions were made.

However, there are more significant similarities in the mode. As a form of invited participation, committee work holds out the promise of bringing members of the public *into* the decision-making processes of a healthcare organisation. By restricting the numbers of participants and engaging them over long periods, the argument is that a more meaningful, informed, and perhaps empowered type of participation can take place. Lay representatives on either existing, or specially convened, committees appear a step closer to Arnstein's (1969) 'citizen control' than citizens who take part in a fleeting consultative outreach project, of the sort I discuss in Chapter 4. The smaller numbers of participants and the more prolonged nature of the interaction seem to create an environment where members of the public can often enjoy what others have described as the non-instrumental benefits of participation: enjoyment, a sense of self-worth, and personal development (Bochel et al 2008).

There are, however, caveats, and 'success' is certainly not clear-cut. One obvious issue relates to the small numbers of individuals who can feasibly be accommodated on practicably sized committees. Clearly, a working committee cannot hope to be a synecdoche of the wider population (Pitkin, 1967). Furthermore, the range of voices and perspectives available is likely limited to those who, by nature or training, are both competent and comfortable in a committee environment. This may bring demographic biases, but equally apparent in my research is the orientation of participants to the organisation. While there might be things they seek to change, their overall disposition to the service they are within tends to be one of significant loyalty and gratitude. Individuals who have more fundamental objections to the organisation, or indeed who are uninterested in it, may occasionally stumble into these opportunities, but rarely endure for long. The public perspectives which we will explore in Chapters 6 and 7 are uncomfortable fits for committee work.

Even where committee work does succeed in feeding a strong and relatively independent 'public' perspective into existing decision-making processes, there is work to do in making space for that perspective. Davies et al.'s (2006, p. 228) ethnographic study of the NICE Citizen's Council in England concluded that 'the work of legitimating and integrating a deliberative assembly into already established institutional structures entails a confrontation both with the assumptions which underpin those structures and with the language which has been developed to sustain them'. In short, all the efforts of 'engager' staff and 'engaged' public committee members cannot guarantee any systemic impact.

A final caveat, or more accurately a second tension within this mode, is the extent to which the public participant's role takes on the characteristics of unpaid work, or volunteering, within the organisation. The bureaucratic requirements for agendas, minutes, and reports to structure and be generated within committee work make such roles potentially burdensome to members of the public. As the example of the Forum above demonstrates, these rituals of bureaucratic life can be gratifying for participants, but they also redirect public energies into conformist behaviour, rather than external critique.

4
Extending the System: Citizen Participation as Outreach Work

Chapter 3 explored committee work in health systems as a mode of participation, arguing that it requires formal bureaucratic skills and a long-term commitment to the organisation, and generates problematic dilemmas around questions of representation. In this chapter we turn to a mode which is to some extent designed to solve these dilemmas, by explicitly aiming to engage as wide a spectrum of the population as possible. What I term outreach work encompasses a wide range of short-term or one-off projects which seek to elicit a wide range of public perspectives on a specific issue. This is the quintessential terrain of contemporary participation, where the lay committee representative or small standing groups discussed in the previous chapter are seen as reliant on too small a section of the population. Methods for 'doing' participation are promoted by organisations such as the International Association for Public Participation, catalogued by Participedia (www. participedia.net), and eagerly adopted by a range of actors including large multinational consultancies (Mann et al 2013). Mitton et al.'s (2009) international scoping review of participation in health found that just under half (49%) of studies reported one-off engagements, rather than ongoing processes. The same review also found that 38% of studies 'reported that particular attention was paid to soliciting the input and participation of disadvantaged populations or groups with special needs' (Mitton et al 2009. p 223).

I consider outreach work to demonstrate four key characteristics. It is short-term (perhaps even one-off) in duration; it requires a fairly minimal contribution, perhaps only a simple statement of opinion or experience; it (therefore) requires some translation or synthesis in order to be used within existing decision-making or governance structures; and it offers no formal authorisation or accountability of citizen to the wider citizenry.

Outreach is often, as in the examples discussed below from Rivermouth, developed explicitly to counter concerns about representation in committee-focused work. Davies et al. (2006, p. 212) discussed the way in which NICE decision-makers gradually moved to supplement the decisions of its deliberative assembly with wider opinion polling: 'polling as a self-evident means, through triangulation, of checking the validity of recommendations made'. Minorities, and groups perceived as 'hard-to-reach' or 'under-represented' by organisations can be targeted to try to broaden the range of voices that are heard (Curtis et al., 2004). However, despite what such projects offer in reach, they can be criticised for sacrificing meaningful engagement and empowerment. At a remove from the town halls and meeting rooms of conventional outreach work, contemporary outreach work also encompasses aspects of what Lupton (2014) describes as the 'digital patient experience economy'. The potential of new technologies/platforms, coupled with the popularity of online feedback sites such as Patient Opinion in the UK (www.patientopinion.org.uk), has generated scope for healthcare organisations to gather opinion from citizens without staff leaving their desks. However, as Lupton (2014, p. 866) cautions in her critique of a 'dominant techno-utopian approach', little is yet known about how members of the public use these facilities, and the uses to which their opinions and narratives are put.

Outreach work at the local level in the Scottish NHS

In the Scottish context, attempts by the Scottish Government to ascertain citizens' views on the NHS have relied on the Better Together patient experience programme (not to be confused with the identically named pro-union campaign in the lead-up to the 2014 independence referendum). This has consisted of highly structured questionnaires, the collection of 'patient stories' volunteered by members of the public, and a limited amount of qualitative research, usually undertaken with hospital inpatients or regular attendees (e.g. those suffering from long-term health conditions) (McKissock, 2008; Reeves, 2008). In one Scottish study, reliance on patient satisfaction questionnaires as a means of 'involvement' was criticised as 'the simplest interpretation and application of involvement and implies no action on the part of services ... nor any indication of partnership or collaboration between patient and professional' (Forbat et al., 2009, p. 2550).

In this chapter, I turn to interviews with staff members responsible for a range of outreach-style participation projects at the local level. While the Public Partnership Forum and other committee work was a key facet of participation in Rivermouth, in the Scottish Health Council' local officer, William, and the Board equalities lead, Linda, I found two people enacting an alternative vision of public involvement. I characterise this approach as 'extending' participation because it stemmed from a basic dissatisfaction with the mainstream, committee-based approach, and a recognition that formal meetings were failing to reach much of the population.

William: Now, one of the difficulties is that if you're having meetings during the day, then you're going to get a predominance of retired people. Because people who are out working, or Mums with families, where do they have the time?

Linda: Because the [Forum] I think are really just getting to grips with [engaging and consulting]. They're still into big events. A lot. But what we need to do is get away from big events and have focus groups. We need to go to where people are already meeting.

Both Linda and William described worries about the diversity of the public being reached by the PPF.

While some concern was expressed about helping the PPF to engage with a broader section of the public, extending public involvement more often looked outside of the statutory mechanisms. The result was a very different understanding of participation. Linda recognised the statutory legitimacy of the PPF, but struggled to reconcile this with other areas of her work where different notions of representation prevailed (Linda: 'It's very easy to say yes we've got groups, and we've got reference groups and we've got web pages, but who sits on these groups?') Outside of the formal public involvement which took place in an orderly, bureaucratic fashion through the PPF, William and Linda both undertook *ad hoc* 'outreach' work with local groups, and advocated moving away from the standalone events-centred approach they associated with the PPF:

William: As opposed to the scattershot approach to the public is the rifle shot approach that says, let's pick 'em off … So I'm convinced that this is the way for us to go, you know, get out there. Not to say, oh, come along, but for us to go and meet them there, where they meet, when they meet, so if it's a weekend, if it's an evening, whatever.

This involved operating at the edge of their administrative job descriptions, and in William's case created something of a tension in his day-to-day workload, which thus included both public-facing outreach work with marginalised groups as a representative of the NHS ('I'm going away to see the Chinese elderly people because there's an issue about diabetes'), and responding to requests from NHS staff as an independent evaluator ('It's something we've been asked to look at'). These projects looked different from committee-work in that they were tailored to 'pick off' particular groups of the population, rather than being designed to answer a pre-defined question. Events were tailored to fit in with existing plans, so were less like a formal meeting:

Linda: You know, if I had a meeting for the deaf society or people, the people who are deaf and actually use British Sign Language, I reckon I'd get none to come along. But if I go along there [to an existing meeting] on a Tuesday night, like they are really pleased to see me, and talk about issues that they're having about accessing our services.

However, the tailoring (William: 'What they wanted was somebody from public health to come along and talk about swine flu. But it's not the big overall arching policies they're interested in. It's about how, what affects their health, at this given time') meant that these events were less suited to feeding into existing decision-making processes. As contact didn't take place within the structure of an existing consultation, there would rarely be a resulting course of action to justify. William said that information gained at these events would contribute to his decisions about signing off the Board's PFPI self-assessment. As a member of Board staff, Linda was able to advocate for changes more directly, without waiting for a review or consultation to feed back through: she used the example of changing hospital rules to allow deaf patients to use mobile phones on ward to send text messages.

Outreach work started by identifying groups who were available and/or under-represented. Instead of the all-affected principle of democratic theory, Linda was concerned to engage with 'equalities groups' as defined by the NHS Scotland equality schemes for disability, gender and ethnicity. In one case, Linda described working with community groups from outside the geographical area in order to develop resources for patients in the area. Here, achieving a successful outcome via accessing 'community' knowledge was defined with no reference to the existing population within Rivermouth. Linda and William exercised significant discretion in identifying these groups, but Linda said she wanted better patient monitoring to allow more rigorous selection of under-represented groups. 'The Chinese elderly' or 'the Polish Association' were both seen as under-represented, but these 'target populations' also had the advantage of being easily accessible through existing associations. Other target groups – such as British Sign Language users – were identified as under-represented by staff and external support was brought in to engage with them. This was the way in which one of the example projects discussed below, of outreach work with young people by health improvement staff and youth workers, was initiated.

Staff accounts pointed to the 'engagement' of young people within the CHP as an additional facet of activity not satisfied through the PPF, and the CHP committee had requested that additional work be done with this group. Health improvement staff and local authority youth workers (Mark, Karen, Pat and Donna) were seen as the key individuals conducting such work. Interviewees talked about four projects in particular. The first was a network of Youth Forums facilitated by youth work staff, described by staff as flexible, *ad hoc* structures led by young people's own interests. Another project, the Debating Project, was planned by health improvement staff as a series of training workshops for young people followed by a debate with local service providers. The Youth Perspectives Project consisted of one-off focus groups with existing groups of vulnerable young people including: young carers; young people excluded from mainstream education; teenage parents; and young people at risk of drug addiction. Finally, health improvement staff ran a Drop-in Service across a range of youth clubs in the area. Staff tailored the drop-in in response to feedback and requests from young people, and accordingly the service broadened beyond sexual health issues to cover all 'teen issues'. This section characterises the outreach work of these staff as translation between service use (and tales thereof) and the governance of the healthcare organisation.

Firstly, 'mini-publics' were assembled. Projects mostly reached younger, school-age people. In some cases this was intentional, as for the Youth Perspectives Project, which targeted 14–18 year olds because 'it is during these middle teenage years that important stages of development occur' (project report) but also for practicality. In others, namely Drop-in Service and the Debating Project, organisers had tried, with limited success, to reach older age groups. In common with the emerging approach for mainstream Rivermouth public involvement, staff tended to work through existing groups rather than trying to recruit from the population at large. This was the case with the Drop-in Service, but also Youth Forums, which worked by formalising groups of young people who were already meeting socially.

Pat: You know, we call it a Youth Forum and sometimes staff get a bit hung up on that and think that a Forum is a definite thing, but that might be a campaigning group, it might be a pressure group, it might be a skate park needed or something and so that's what we call these Forums, em, so it's shorthand really for where these people come together.

Staff described a number of advantages to this approach; it was quicker and meant that the expertise of existing support workers was available. However, they also acknowledged that working with or through existing groups had its tensions, including imposing external (NHS) priorities on to groups who exist for other purposes, such as respite for young carers.

All interviewees preferred working with small groups of familiar young people. Frontline members of staff, working in the Drop-in Service and in Youth Forums, described knowing groups of young people well and working with them repeatedly across different projects:

Karen: A lot of them knew my face, so it was quite easy. That's, recruitment was not a problem.

This trust enabled Karen to draw together groups in response to requests from other agencies, sometimes at short notice.

Karen: So, I got an email, and they had like a week to make [a consultation event]. So, em, [named group of young people], yet again, you know because I had this lot's email addresses fired it off to them 'who can attend?'... They were there, at the railway station, at 7 o'clock on a Saturday morning, knowing they should still have been wrapped up in their beds, but keen as mustard to go along.

Karen describes the pragmatic way – last minute requests, convenient channels of communication – in which groups of 'usual suspects' emerge in youth engagement. Sometimes these young people went on to stand for election to the Scottish Youth Parliament, and this led to being in considerable demand to sit on various NHS and local authority committees. Where this trust – or at least familiarity – was absent, it was seen as a major obstacle to engagement (Karen: 'It would have to be sort of cold-calling just as they're walking in and out type of thing, trying to get them, and if you're not a known face, that's sometimes really difficult').

Views were often gathered through projects with a developmental focus familiar from community development approaches. The Debating Project is a good example; young people worked through a 'pack' with health improvement staff before preparing for the meeting with senior staff.

Karen: Em, and it basically gets them just to, initially gets them to look at, you know, what they think are issues for them. And then it gets them to think, well, if that's an issue, why is it an issue?

This was described as a respectful process, working with expressed views and exploring them further. Nonetheless Donna's comment that one of the Youth Perspectives Project focus groups was 'maybe not as controlled, or as tight as I would have liked it to have been' hints at the disciplining force of these ongoing relationships, which helped young people to articulate views on services within the confines of the existing system. Staff described trying to strike a balance between giving young people control and helping them to express views effectively. Pat described how one youth forum had come up with a proposal to produce a booklet for distribution at a cost of £9 per copy, at which point staff had intervened to come up with a more affordable alternative.

The other side of outreach work was using known information about young people's views, 'needs' and experiences to influence the local management of services. Staff described a number of facets of this influence: frontline staff and youth representatives sitting on committees; bringing together groups of young people with local politicians or service managers; and information-sharing through reports and presentations. The role of frontline staff in advocating for young people's perspectives has been highlighted, and indeed defended, in other literature. Macpherson's (2008) study of socially excluded young people highlighted the potential of specialist youth workers representing their clients' views in partnership committees, and the difficulties encountered by such staff: 'In stepping outside the adult world and aligning themselves with young people, advocates confuse their peers' (Macpherson, 2008, p. 374). Karen talked about this in less dramatic terms as becoming 'a pest' ('we're always telling other people how they should treat young people'). Health improvement staff described their own role on committees as a key mechanism of influence, heavily informed by their own frontline and consultative work. Donna described consultation work as assurance for her that the committees she sat on were working on the right issues.

Other projects worked by bringing young people into direct engagement with service providers and politicians. Mark described workshop-type events as the best way to influence service providers, but both he and Karen emphasised the challenges of creating a dialogue with suspicion on both sides:

Mark: And there's key councillors who have a general interest in young people and will come along and they're very good with young people. There's others that are interested in hearing about young people, but won't engage with them; they'll just sort of sit back.

Karen: They just felt they would be palmed off. They thought [service providers] would have time to think about it and come up with a smarmy answer that was ... They really wanted to get reactions and get them on the spot. They really liked it. The service providers really didn't like being put on the spot. So it was one of those things.

Engagement staff operated as a conduit, trusted to some extent both by young people and the decision makers.

An additional mechanism of influence came from the reports which were produced for each project. These were seen as a key output of the projects by interviewees, and I came away from each interview with a pile of reports. For the Youth Perspective Project, a 50-page report had been produced. The main sections of the report included an analysis of themes from focus groups, using short quotes to exemplify each theme. Many quotes are in local youth vernacular, and several are provocative (for example, 'get rid of old grannies' 'kill the junkies'). A warning about this is added to the section 'research objectives and methods':

'Comments have, in virtually all cases, been taken at face value. It is inevitable, however, that some comments would have been made to try to shock the facilitator, or to show off to friends. The analysis has not attempted to differentiate these comments and uses virtually all of the material gathered. Readers should note that direct quotations are presented within this document which some people may consider offensive.'

This can be seen as an example of the challenges facing 'engagers' in mediating between the informally expressed, unorganised speech of young adults and the formal committee structures which wait to hear their 'voice'. The final two sections use no direct quotes and transform the fragmented themes of earlier sections into 'key messages' and recommendations. To exemplify disconnects within this process, I attempted to trace each of the six bullet-pointed recommendations back through the key messages into the themes section. For example:

Recommendation:	'Building on good practice established within the Board area, sustain, support and further develop the Family Health Project. This project comprises of Family Health Midwives and Nursery Nurses providing enhanced support to vulnerable groups, including teenage parents.'
Key message:	'Midwives were regarded as a key support during pregnancy.'
Theme:	'With the exception of lack of sleep, and to some extent, anxiety arising from concerns about their children, there were no health issues raised. Generally, midwives were viewed very positively, although doctors were not regarded particularly well.'

This example is chosen because it is more specific and thus traceable than others (for example: 'Continue to engage and involve young people in planning and developing responsive health improvement initiatives'). However, it demonstrates the process of taking messy statements from focus group participants, ironing out some of the inconsistencies ('Generally, midwives were viewed very positively' becomes 'regarded as a key support') and fitting them into the known decision-making context of the CHP ('regarded as a key support' becomes a recommendation to develop a project that does not appear to have been mentioned by any participant). Here, frontline staff used their own knowledge of 'what works' in supporting teenage mothers to translate uncertain, vague statements into clear-cut recommendations with clear actions for the organisation. Within this document, the fault lines in the assemblage of 'public involvement' – the absence of shared meaning which is comprehensible for both 'ordinary' young adults and the committees which seek their views – become visible.

One reason for this process of translation was that the views elicited from young people did not fit neatly into the questions asked or decisions being made within the Rivermouth CHP. Sometimes this was because views crossed into the terrain of other public services.

Donna: Things about their environment, things maybe about that there's nothing to do in the evenings, and all these types of things that the NHS maybe not directly would have an influence over, but certainly sitting on strategic groups and partnership groups we could work with the partners to maybe address.

However, it also related to the broad, societal nature of challenges identified. For the health improvement staff, this was an intrinsic challenge of the broad understanding of health with which they worked:

Donna: You're sitting with young people, 'what do you mean health?' 'Oh I eat pizza and I do this' so it was about spending a wee bit time to say 'well health is much more than that, it's what makes you happy, what makes you sad, how do you feel about this?' ... I knew what I wanted to get, but as soon as young people hear health, they think pizza, chips, that type of stuff.

Here, Donna describes the process of moving beyond instinctive 'gut' reactions to questions about health, to the broader wellbeing focus of much health improvement ('I knew what I wanted to get'). Having transformed young people's focus on their own actions into a 'health improvement' focus on environmental and societal contributions, Donna was left with some remarkably broad-sweep conclusions. This necessitated an approach of picking small achievable actions out of the broad scope of consultation:

Donna: We've produced this report ... and obviously there's, there are recommendations that come from it that are fairly broad, em, but what is a result of it is that I now have a work plan where I'm going to try to progress some of this work forward, em, and hopefully, drive some improvements where maybe found, I don't know, we found one or two things that maybe could be looked at or work around a specific topic.

Sometimes, by contrast, recommendations seemed troublesome because they sounded trivial when placed within the context of local health services management. Talking about GP practices and the recommendations of *Walk the Talk*, a national project, Karen explained:

Karen: They're just, it's always like, em, like you go in and it'll be golf magazines and like women's weekly or something, you know ... One of the *Walk the Talk* recommendations is to sort of make them a bit more young people friendly.

In Rivermouth, health improvement staff operated as a two-way conduit for young people's views. They advocated for young people's priorities in NHS and local authority committees, but they also reflected understanding of what is and isn't acceptable or achievable back to the spaces in which they coached and shaped young adults' views. I understand this not as a malign or repressive act, but as a pragmatic response to the gap between the way young adults spontaneously discuss their health and the way in which health service management decisions are made. This reflects the distinction that Yanow (1996, p. xiii) makes between organisational processes as 'rational-technical', compared with more mundane, 'messy' lived experiences. Public involvement creates demand for the experiences of service users to be brought into these 'rational' and technical settings. Accordingly, practitioners such as Donna, Karen, and Mark find themselves in the position of needing to enact a process of translation: 'a sense of doing something other or more than merely telling, of communicative and perhaps creative exchanges rather than dissemination' (Freeman, 2009, p. 441).

Outreach as a mode of participation

In the introduction to this chapter I briefly suggested four key characteristics which identify outreach work as a mode of interaction between health systems and their publics. This section takes these further, reflecting on their implications for outreach practices, participants, and organisations. A first, and crucial, defining feature of outreach work as a mode of public engagement in health systems is that it proceeds primarily through one-off or short-term projects. These are generally initiated within the healthcare organisation to meet a perceived need, whether that be canvassing the views of a local population on some specific service change, or on 'hearing from' a specific group within the population. They are not designed to provide a 'standing' forum for engagement, and accordingly the time commitment required is usually short, and can be as little as attending an event or complete a form online.

As well as asking for a relatively small time commitment, these opportunities tend to ask very little of participants in terms of analytic work or translating their own experiences into the decision-making framework of the relevant organisation. Designed usually to hear from members of the public, they will often address a set of pre-defined questions or ask simply 'what are your experiences of *x*'. While deliberative events such as citizens' juries (Coote and Lenaghan, 1997) might demand a more thoroughgoing engagement, because these are carefully facilitated events it is possible for members of the public to contribute without committing to onerous or time-consuming work outside of the 'moment' of engagement.

However, because members of the public are generally given freer rein within these participatory spaces, it is also the case that outreach work will not often yield findings which can be neatly fed in to existing decision-making processes. Where a committee might be ruminating on a possible change of strategy for a specific community service, outreach projects tend to gather views at a more micro, experiential level. (Projects which aspire to engage members of the public in producing a more formal response to an issue may well shift into the category of committee work, rather than outreach.)

Partly as a result of this likely mismatch between what members of the public will spontaneously discuss and how large healthcare organisations make decisions, another defining feature of outreach is that it often requires a substantial cadre of skilled professional 'engagers' of the sort described ethnographically in the Scottish context by Escobar (2014), or in the American context by Eliasoph (2011). These individuals are employed to undertake careful facilitation of events ('scripting', as Escobar depicts it) and then the translation of gathered views into formalised outputs which can be fed into decision-making processes ('inscription', for Escobar). An interesting variant of this is online 'patient experience' platforms such as Patient Opinion and Dr Foster, which, Lupton argues, are particularly valued because of the ostensible absence of a mediating human being: 'the beliefs that digital data are neutral, unmediated, and clean forms of knowledge because they are produced by computerised systems, and that the more data, the better' (Lupton, 2014, p. 859). In both cases, the mediating role needs to demonstrate its *lack* of influence, in order to render the outputs 'representative', while nonetheless exerting enough influence to ensure that those outputs remain 'useful'.

Finally, while often initiated specifically to tackle concerns around equality, diversity, and representation within healthcare decision-making, outreach projects still offer no formal accountability between public and participants. Indeed, it could be argued that the one-off nature of engagement and the greater encouragement to simply 'speak for oneself' without reference to a wider imagined public makes this an even less representative mode of engagement in the political sense. However, in Martin's (2008b) 'descriptive/statistical' sense of representativeness, outreach far outperforms committee work. Finding an individual whose demographic characteristics or experiential credentials can 'tick' a specific box is vastly easier where the overall numbers of engaged citizens are higher, and where the time and effort commitment is lower. In the next chapter we turn to a mode with an entirely different approach to questions of representation; representative democracy.

5
Electing the System: Citizen Participation as Representative Democracy

Having, in Chapters 3 and 4, discussed the invited modes by which healthcare organisations seek to engage their publics, this chapter turns instead to the opportunities created by the intersection of local structures of representative democracy and health systems. The role of representative democracy is rarely in the foreground within much health services literature, where healthcare organisations are often depicted as looking 'up' to faceless regulators and managers, and 'down' to their publics and service users, with minimal discussion of the political contexts which frame both of these relationships.

In publicly funded health systems, and especially in NHS systems like Scotland, the institutions of representative democracy frame the provision of healthcare. Publicly funded health systems have historically operated on a basic model of central government accountability. A central government Minister for Health (or an equivalent title) thus holds ultimate responsibility for the organisations that deliver healthcare to the population. In the early days of the UK NHS, Bevan famously declared: 'The Minister of Health will be whipping-boy for the Health Service in Parliament. Every time a maid kicks over a bucket of slops in a ward an agonised wail will go through Whitehall' (2009, p. 179). This bold statement now, however, bears little resemblance to contemporary governance structures. The multiplication of organisations who plan, provide, and regulate health services is, if not actually intended to dilute ministerial responsibility, surely the death knell of any practicable notion of it (Peckham et al., 2005). Organisations are often run by appointees of the Minister, who is accountable to parliament, who are held accountable by voters in elections. Both the sheer complexity of modern health systems, and perhaps an enhanced appreciation of the difficulties of the task of ensuring high-quality provision to a population

with changing health needs, have made central government accountability both practically challenging and politically undesirable.

Health policy in the UK has been concerned to establish other
avenues for redress and influence than direct control by central government since at least the 1970s (Klein and Lewis, 1976).This has often
been accompanied by repeated attempts to decentralise power, and thus
responsibility, to intermediate organisations including 'quangos' or
non-departmental public bodies (Klein, 2010). Such moves have almost
invariably included the creation of the type of citizen participation
initiatives which I discussed in Chapters 3 and 4, and which Warren
(2009a) argues draw their rationale from deliberative and participatory
models of democracy. This also reflects wider trends beyond health
systems, whereby advocates of 'more' democracy have concentrated on
supplementing representative democracy with participatory or deliberative initiatives, rather than extending or reforming representative
structures (Urbinati and Warren, 2008; Warren, 2009b). However, there
are exceptions to this, both in the UK and internationally. Two main
options for enhanced representative democratic control of health systems are strengthening the control of existing local-level elected authorities, or creating 'new' health-specific elected authorities at local level.

The Nordic healthcare systems are the archetypal example of
devolved local authority responsibility (and in some cases tax-raising
powers) for healthcare (Martinussen and Magnussen, 2009). More
recent research points to significant and increasing diversity within this
group of countries (Magnussen et al., 2009), and to a more complex
picture of multi-level governance of healthcare (Hagen and Vrangbaek,
2009). However, it remains true that, in comparison to NHS models,
there is a far greater role for elected local and regional governments in
these countries. Longstanding questions about whether elected local
authorities should have more control over health services in the UK
have been reinvigorated in recent years by issues around the integration
of health and (local authority-managed) social care. That the NHS has
never been under local authority control is a consequence of the 1940
political settlement ('a monument to the conflicting views of the pressure groups' (Hudson, 1998, p. 73)). Writing two years after the major
1974 reorganisation of the UK NHS, Klein and Lewis (1976, p. 12)
argued that introducing some measure of local level 'consumer representation' via the Community Health Councils was a tactic to avoid
the 'theoretically desirable but politically impracticable' option of local
government control of health services. The 1990 reforms created further
distance between local authorities and healthcare (Hudson, 1998), but

from 1997 a stronger role for local government was developed, with the explicit goal of enhancing accountability to the public (Coleman and Glendinning, 2004). Formal scrutiny of local health services by local authority Overview and Scrutiny Committees commenced in England and Wales in 2001. This measure can be understood, Harrison and McDonald (2008, p. 123) argue, as 'the means of tying-up local politicians in the formidable technical detail of health issues'. In 2012, Labour Shadow Health Secretary Andy Burnham again proposed a merged 'national health and care service', broadly supported by the findings of the Barker Commission, but the required structural changes may prove politically unpalatable in the current climate.

The alternative approach of creating health-specific elected authorities is one which has been adopted (and in some cases subsequently abandoned) in New Zealand and some Canadian provinces, as well as in Scotland (Stewart et al., 2015). In New Zealand, directly elected boards have run first hospitals and then (on-and-off) district health boards since before a national health service existed (Laugesen and Gauld, 2012). Elected boards were also created in a number of Canadian provinces as part of a wider programme of regionalisation beginning in the 1990s (Church and Barker, 1998). While all were later abandoned in the 2000s, New Brunswick reintroduced elections in 2012. England's Foundation Trust hospitals have included an elected board within their rather complicated governance structures since 2004 (Allen et al., 2012; Day and Klein, 2005). The key arguments in favour of creating elected boards generally invoke elections as the ultimate test of democratic popular control, and point to the logistical obstacles to simply handing health services over to already-elected local authorities. Each system which has experimented with elections has been plagued by concerns about turnout, levels of candidacy (i.e. the risk of uncontested elections) and the significant financial costs of creating and running an additional tier of elections (Stewart et al., 2015). It is telling that New Zealand, the system with the longest history of elected boards, is the one country where pragmatic concerns about costs and public appetite for elections do not seem to outweigh more principled demands for elections (Gauld, 2005). The efforts needed to mandate elections and sustain them through the early years of establishment appear to be particularly politically challenging.

In practice, structures of representative democracy within healthcare are both rapidly shifting and more complex than the theoretical lines of accountability might suggest. This chapter explores two recent examples within the landscape of the Scottish NHS since devolution. The first is the inclusion of elected councillors on Health Boards, and in the next section I review the history of this policy in the Scottish context and draw on interview data to explore the 'public-facing' elements of this specific role. The second is a short-lived policy pilot, where in 2010 direct elections were held for a majority of members of two Health Boards.

Local elected politicians on Scottish Health Boards

As discussed in Chapter 2, 'strengthening the voice' of local government on Health Boards has been on the agenda in this area since unified territorial Health Boards were announced in 2000 (Scottish Executive, 2000). This evolved into a convention that Health Boards would include councillors from local authorities on their boards, which was then put on a statutory footing in the Health Boards (Membership and Election) Act 2009 (the same act that legislated the pilot elections discussed below). This stated that each Board should include 'councillors appointed by the Scottish Ministers following nomination by local authorities in the area of the Health Board ("councillor members")' and that 'a Board must contain at least one councillor member for each local authority whose area is wholly or partly within the area of the Board' (*Health Boards (Membership and Elections) (Scotland) Act*, 2009).

By convention, this is generally either (with allowances for varying terminology in different authorities) the Leader of the Council, or the Councillor who chairs the local authority's social work committee.

Partly because of the gradual evolution of this measure and the multiple aims of the policy (concerned both with democratic accountability and more practical questions around the integration of health and social care) the nature of the role played by councillors on the Health Boards is not entirely clear. It is certainly not primarily understood as a move to protect the public voice within the NHS. Public sector trade union UNISON described the role thus:

> The appointment of councillors to health boards was primarily done to recognise the key role local authorities have in promoting better health and the importance of joined up services through initiatives like Joint Future. Most councillors on health boards therefore see their primary role as representing their council, not as some form of directly elected member.
>
> (UNISON Scotland, 2008)

There was some evidence for this in interviews conducted with eight local authority councillor members in 2010–2011. In most cases, being nominated as the local authority 'stakeholder member' on the Board was simply a secondary consequence of taking a particular role within the council.

Councillor 1:   It's chance that I've ended up on [the Board] because of my position on [the council] … I was interested in taking a senior role and therefore being part of the sort of senior elected member team, because I'm involved in terms of driving policy across the board as a senior elected member. I was going to say that [social care] was the one that nobody else wanted but that's perhaps not quite true.

One notable exception, which was mentioned by councillors from a range of authorities and Boards, was one local authority where a local 'save the hospital' campaigner was first elected as a local councillor and then, when his party unexpectedly held the balance of power on the council, nominated as the council's stakeholder member on the Board. This nomination was disputed by the Board, and after what one councillor described as 'fisticuffs', the Minister intervened to support the council's nomination. This unusual situation seemed to highlight a range of tensions in the respective roles and power bases of elected local authorities and appointed Health Boards, and it elicited strong reactions from several councillors:

Councillor 2:   I think, in fact, the fisticuffs had to take place because of the intransigence of the board in May by first of all challenging a democratically elected body, in West Lothian council. Which makes a nominee to go to the minister for a seat on the board. So it's in my view not the role of the health board to actually challenge a council decision. It's for the minister to decide…

Councillor 3:   That was ridiculous. The board doesn't appoint itself. How dare they!

In this case, the nomination of an individual with a clear and highly politicised mandate to pursue a particular agenda provoked a confrontational response from a Board more comfortable with a conventional role focused on liaison with social care.

However, barring this challenging example, the issue of who or what councillors were meant to represent on the Board was not one on which most interviewees had strong pre-formed views.

Interviewer: What do you see as your role in that, where you're rep-
                resenting the council but you're also appointed by the
                minister, you're elected by the population?

Councillor 1:   Good question. Part of the answer is I don't compart-
                mentalise myself and think in different ways – perhaps
                I should.

Several interviewees stated that their eventual accountability was to
the electorate; not of their specific council ward, but of everyone in the
NHS Board area.

Councillor 1:   I actually think all members of the board should say
                'I am representing the people of [Board area]', I mean
                I happen to have been the one who has been elected.

Councillor 4:   That's easy, because it's the public. It's the public,
                whichever hat I'm wearing. They're the ones that I've
                got to answer to, in the long term ... I'm responsible
                to the minister, but beyond that, as a public servant,
                I'm responsible to the public. And it's their taxes that
                pay my wages. And that's how I kind of keep it in
                mind.

By contrast, other interviewees denied this, stating clearly that their
appointment, and thus allegiance, was with the Minister.

Interviewer: Who would you see yourself as being accountable to for
                the work you do on the board?

Councillor 5:   To the minister.

Interviewer: Not to the electorate?

Councillor 5:   No. I'm appointed by, it's a ministerial appointment.
                So we're answerable to the minister.

Councillor 6:   I am very much aware that as somebody involved in
                politics, I have signed up for the Board to help imple-
                ment NHS policy as determined by the government, but
                the government are not my political party. I'm there as
                a non-exec director.

In more practical terms, interviewees described their role on Boards in a
number of different ways. The most common role described was simply
that of a 'bridge between the two organisations' (Councillor 4).

Councillor 1:   The council nominees have a very particular role, and they are there to facilitate the local authority and the health board. And that's defined in the guidance from the Scottish government as to how that should be done. And I mean I'm very, especially at a time of financial crisis and a time of sharing services, we've got to ensure that that level of communication is highly effective.

All interviewees agreed that this was an important and increasingly necessary role as the demands of an ageing population required both more, and better, joint working between health and social care services.

There were, however, two alternative understandings to the 'bridge' or 'conduit' role between the two organisations. Several interviewees downplayed this information exchange role, describing themselves more as another non-executive (with commensurate responsibilities for scrutiny).

Councillor 1:   If I'm honest, I rarely go back to the two political groups, I'm almost going to be struggling to think of issues where if you like I went back to the political groups and said there's this big issue coming up at the health board next week, you know, what do you want me to do? How do you want me to vote?

Councillor 2:   I find the terminology dinosauric really. You either have executive members and nonexecutive members, and that's really the route of travel. The difference between a lay member and stakeholder member has never crossed my path before. There's never anybody who's said 'well I'm a lay member'. It's just a different route of being appointed.

Alternatively, one interviewee argued instead that their role was a one-way defence of the council's interests on the Board:

Councillor 3:   I'm the council's bod in the NHS, I'm not the NHS's person on the council. So I have to look out for the council's interests. I think I've largely played a very constructive role.

The specifically political, public-facing dimensions of elected politicians were also relevant here, in offering scrutiny, but from a specific angle:

Councillor 3:   Your job is to hold these directors to account and to make sure that you're providing a different take on things. Experts are experts, but they don't always have context. Managers will always want to manage, and not always in a way that's sensitive to public opinion.

Whether or not councillors brought a specifically 'public' perspective onto Boards was a complex and somewhat divisive question. Few interviewees said that members of the public brought issues to them as a Board member.

Interviewer: Do people actually get in touch with you?
Councillor 7: Yes. Not as often as they do with the councillor hat on, but people have been known to get in touch with me. Particularly when there are difficult decisions to be made ... [Specific consultation] That's the most public contact that I've had. And they were lobbying the board right left and centre. They were lobbying everyone they could lay their hands on ... And they were lobbying me as a member of the board. I mean obviously the councillors were kind of the first target, but no, they were writing to all members of the board they were emailing all members of the board.

However, several felt that their strong connections to and visibility with their constituents were assets to the Boards:

Councillor 8: I'm in contact with a lot of people across [the area], and I think that's important, I'm exposed to lots of people's thoughts on what's happening with [services here].

This did not, however, in most cases equate to playing a lobbying role in Board meetings. If a councillor wished to raise an individual constituent's problem 'I would wait until the lunch break or coffee break and I might go and have a word with somebody' (Councillor 1).

Rather, the 'corporate responsibility' of the Board required stakeholder members, as with other members, to stand behind collective decisions.

Councillor 5: On the one hand you can express freely and strongly the views that you get in your community ... But when the decision is made you have to accept the strategic, collective decision. And you would have to defend it. Otherwise the board would fall to bits if we were all running around making territorial decisions…

Despite a willingness to 'toe the line' on Boards and adopt a broadly conventional non-executive role, most interviewees noted the differences in organisational culture between the local authority and the NHS Board, in particular as regards the relationship with the public. The low numbers and decorous conduct of public attendees at Board meetings was contrasted with the 'hundreds' who would attend council meetings and 'heckle' unpopular decisions. Most interviewees agreed that Boards were, on balance, less engaged with, open to, and comfortable with their publics than local authorities.

Councillor 3:   I think they tick all the boxes that are required. They will hold all the necessary meetings. I'm not sure that underneath that there's a genuine sense that public engagement is something that's there to change decision-making. I think it's more a case of we will meet the public and tell them what we're doing. I start from a different perspective from my local government experience and things, and the way we approach things. Again a different culture. But you'd be hard placed to – all the boxes will be ticked and on paper it will look like genuine public involvement or engagement has taken place.

Several interviewees also, with some pride, described their comfort with the 'rough and tumble' of public interaction, specifically on divisive issues, and contrasted this with Board member discomfort with highly public decisions.

Councillor 8:   You know as a council member I'm used to the public having access to me. If they disagree with me you know you'll get heckled at a meeting or whatever. And the board doesn't have that … The board don't like confrontation … [In a specific public meeting] You know, people rushing at me doesn't really bother me. But some of them found it very very intimidating that people were actually disagreeing with them. They hadn't experienced that. So public meetings where there's controversial issues, they didn't like that. I actually, you know, quite like that sort of confrontation. And I think they were like rabbits in headlights ...

Interviews with councillor members of Health Boards thus suggested an uncertain, shifting role in which they had to balance the different interests and working styles of two very different types of organisations. There was no consensus as to whether these 'stakeholder members' were simply a non-executive member with an unusual mode of appointment, a representative of their council, there to protect its interests, or a simple form of information exchange, to ease the challenges of joint working. As politically engaged, publicly visible individuals used to working under considerable scrutiny from public opinion, they offered a very particular perspective on the different working style of NHS Boards. The next section explores another instance in which the structures and culture of representative democracy intersected with the corporate decision-making of these Boards: 2010's pilot direct elections for Health Board members.

The Scottish Health Board election pilots of 2010

Scotland's Health Boards have long been run by appointed boards who are responsible for the planning and provision of almost all health services in their areas. In common with many boards of public bodies, they operate in the realms of 'strategy' and 'governance'. In practice they operate somewhere between the stewardship and principal/agent models of management (Cornforth, 2005), overseeing the actions of professional managers and making particularly important or high-profile decisions. They are not supposed to involve themselves in 'operational matters', and nor, in practice, have Scottish NHS Board members generally fulfilled an 'external role' (Skelcher, 1998, p. 104) dealing with the public and other stakeholders, except in a quasi-ceremonial figurehead capacity – for example appearing in photos at 'turf-cutting' ceremonies for new facilities. This is broadly consistent with the 'expert' mode of working identified in NHS Boards in other areas of the UK, where Board members have minimal dealings with the public as part of their roles (Veronesi and Keasey, 2011, 2010).

Board members for the Health Boards are appointed via the standard public appointments procedures in Scotland. Organisations advertise for board members and the applicant pool is then narrowed using a 'skills matrix', which specifies required skills, such as finance or expertise with corporate governance. The applicants are interviewed by a separate agency, the Office of the Commissioner of Public Appointments in Scotland, and their reports of the interviews are summarised by civil servants before being presented to ministers to select appointees. The posts are part-time, and remunerated at around £8,000 per annum.

The SNP included direct elections to Scottish Health Boards in their 2007 manifesto. Once in power, the then Health Secretary Nicola Sturgeon was a strong supporter of the policy, stating publicly that it would stop Boards being 'able to ride roughshod over community opinion, as has happened in the past' (quoted in The Scottish Government, 2009). Legislation with broad cross-party support was enacted to pilot the direct election of boards, and two boards were selected to hold pilot elections. Elections took place in 2010 by postal vote, using the Single Transferable Vote system with the whole of each board area as a single ward. Candidates were allowed to put themselves forward with a 250-word election address (in which campaign promises and references to party affiliations were acceptable). Election expenditures were limited to £250. Voting packs, sent to all eligible voters, included the election statements and a ballot paper. The elected members, together with local councillors nominated by local authorities and appointed by Ministers, created a majority on both boards. The rest of each board was, as previously, composed of Executive Directors (NHS managers on the board, such as the Chief Executive and Medical Director) and a few remaining appointed non-executives.

The elections created two distinct channels for potential public engagement with the Boards. One was around voting (that the opportunity for members of the public to express a preference would reshape the type of people on Boards) and another was around the ongoing relationships between Board members and publics, and the extent to which these were different for elected members as compared to the appointed members they replaced.

Voting

In order to combat the fear that elections would allow vested interests to capture boards, political party involvement in the actual elections was minimal. However, this also meant that most candidates did not have access to established mechanisms for mobilising public opinion (and for voters' ability to use conventional 'heuristic' shortcuts when choosing between candidates (Wilson et al., 2015)).

Turnout overall was 22.6% in Dumfries and Galloway, and 13.9% in Fife. While low, this is not extreme in comparison with the most recent local authority elections in Scotland (where average turnout was 39.7% (Liddell et al., 2012)). A survey of those registered to vote in the elections suggested that, rather than deprivation, gender, state of health, or disability, the decision to vote was best predicted by the age of the potential voter (Greer et al., 2014b). The official election records showed that turnout among registered electors under 18 was as low as 7% in Fife, and focus groups with 16- and 17-year-olds suggested minimal interest in or awareness of the elections having taken place (Stewart et al., 2014b). This was, as Greer et al. put it, 'an election dominated by the old' (Greer et al., 2014b, p. 1096).

The same research suggested that many potential voters felt very poorly informed about the purpose and process of the election (Greer et al., 2014b). Voters interviewed could not name Board members, even after the elections, unless they happened to be acquaintances or relatives, and most had little sense of what the governing boards actually did. Information for the election mostly consisted of the booklet of candidate statements, sent out as part of voting packs. However, these 250-word statements from each of the candidates offered little help, because the large number of candidates meant that the booklets ran to over 10,000 words and electors had little sense of what criteria they should use to pick a non-executive (Wilson et al., 2015).

The pilot elections took place just a few weeks after the 2010 UK General Election, and comparing how informed voters felt about the two ballots showed a stark contrast, with 27% (Dumfries & Galloway) and 42% (Fife) of voters stating they were 'not at all well informed' about the health board election, compared to 5% (Dumfries & Galloway) and 6% (Fife) about the General Election (Greer et al., 2014b). Voters remained uninformed about the organisation for which they were selecting candidates, which is understandable given Health Boards' lack of public exposure, and most had little information about the candidates. Accordingly, the extent to which the simple act of voting can be understood as a meaningful opportunity for engagement is limited. Voting was a brief, minority pursuit in these pilot elections, which (given low levels of information) offered little opportunity for members of the public to convey their knowledge and preferences for their local healthcare organisations. The unsatisfactory nature of the elections as a moment of 'authorisation' (Greer et al., 2014b) also had consequences for the extent to which those members elected to Boards sought a distinctively 'democratic' relationship with their publics, as compared to their appointed predecessors.

The public role of elected members

In interviews we were able to compare the self-perceived role of appointed Board members with the elected members who replaced or joined them. Generally, appointed members had a fairly uncomplicated understanding of their role on the Boards. They understood themselves as representatives of central government, overseeing Board business from the perspective of government priorities and standards.

Appointed Non-exec 20:   Making sure we're doing the right things mean we have to be aware of government policy. As appointed non-execs we are required to support government policy.

Appointed Non-exec 22:   My responsibility ultimately, as I see it, is to the person who appointed me, who is the minister.

While for many appointed members this was, as in the principal–agent model, a technical business of knowing policy (for example, targets set by central government) and measuring performance against it, a few appointed members highlighted the congruence between current government policy and their own views on health.

Appointed Non-exec 12:   I see my role on the Board as to promote a vision of healthcare that is for me, most succinctly described in *Better Health, Better Care*.

Others still acknowledged a dual burden of responsibility, both to local publics served by the NHS *and* to central government:

Appointed Non-exec 10:   Your role is to understand the health service and its relationship first of all to the people that it serves and then as important is the relationship between the territorial board and the Scottish health department, and the government and its policies.

For a few members, this commitment to the NHS's patients entailed a willingness to proactively criticise and question central government policy:

Appointed Non-exec 1:   We have a strong, well-developed sense that what we do first and foremost is what's right for the health of the citizens of [this area]. The government's targets very often can get in the way of that.

By contrast, elected members were significantly less likely to have a straightforward singular understanding of their role as representing government on the Board. Part of this was a degree of confusion about the legal basis of their accountability:

Elected Non-exec 16: Of course the Board is legally responsible to the Cabinet Secretary, but who are the individual members accountable to? No clear answer, and in my opinion if I'm elected by the people I'm accountable to the people because they are the people that put me here, but that's not the way it works.

Elected Non-exec 16: [Executive members] won't do anything that might be deemed contentious without briefing the Head of the Health Service of Scotland who naturally liaises with the Cabinet Secretary. So although we might be elected, we can't just go off on our own, not that you'd want to do that anyway, I mean you've got to apply common sense here because you're trying to get things done and it's no' necessarily a desirable situation to find yourself in conflict with the Cabinet Secretary ... So you try and avoid that but that question still hangs there 'who are we accountable to?'

In some cases, the relational pull between public and government was rationalised by reference to the government's position as elected representatives of the public:

Elected Non-exec 13: Because you're on the Board you are very much accountable to the population to provide the best services that we're allowed to do so with the money etc. that comes down. But you're eventually accountable to the population through the government because the government has been elected by the population.

This interviewee describes his or her own elected legitimacy as secondary to that of the elected central government. All elected members acknowledged the context of government policy as framing and delimiting Board options:

Elected Non-exec 17:   I mean to some extent you're limited in that the government lays down the targets and the various different things like, you know, sort of breastfeeding and that sort of thing, and while you can, from knowledge and medical knowledge, basic knowledge, know that the particular target might not make sense, the chances of shifting that are very difficult.

Some members went further, expressing surprise (and consternation) at the lack of freedom Boards had to define their own approach:

Elected Non-exec 12:   I didn't realise that Health Boards [were] quite so restricted with government policy, I think that's the first thing that I honestly did not realise. I really thought that Health Boards had more autonomy and they're not, you know, they're very much in a straitjacket. I mean they're limited with resources and they're limited with government, whichever colour of government happen to be in. I hadn't quite realised that so I think ... I thought that I would have been able to make more difference.

One particularly oppositional member, who had campaigned for election with a promise to fight hospital closures in the area, resigned from the Board in order to stand for a Scottish Parliament seat, frustrated at the lack of progress on the Board.

A potential role representing the public put a spotlight on the mechanisms by which Board members engaged with the public. For most appointed members this was work which fell into the 'operational' (as opposed to strategic) realm, and not part of their role.

Appointed Non-exec 9:   I don't think it's my job to go out and canvas what other people think and then come back and say that. I don't believe that's why I've been employed. I believe I've been employed to bring my knowledge and my skills.

A few appointed members went further, stating that they felt that a concern with public acceptability was hampering Boards' ability to deliver effective services.

Others felt simply that their own informal conversations with acquaintances and personal knowledge ensured that they were a 'voice for the public'. In these cases, any queries received would be referred to the appropriate member of staff to be resolved:

Appointed Non-exec 11:   I am a member of the public, I talk to people as I go around the place .... I would feed those in, probably not at a Board meeting but through discussions with appropriate executive colleagues.

A few appointed members understood this connection more holistically, as being about embodying an outsider perspective which was inevitably closer to the public's views.

Appointed Non-exec 6:   We provide a different standpoint. We come I think from a different angle. I'd like to think that we can say, well, have you thought of this or that, and that perhaps someone who is working in something as their job, it's slightly more difficult for them to understand what it looks like to someone standing outside the organisation. So I think we're a kind of a bridge, I'd like to think I'm a bridge between the public and the organisation.

By contrast, the nature of their accountability to and engagement with the public preoccupied most elected members.

Elected Non-exec 11:   It is that difference between election and appointment in that had people not, you know, voted for me I wouldn't have been elected and they have done so and I feel some responsibility to the people who have elected me.

Elected Non-exec 7:   [I] try and speak to as many people as I could and I've got links into my local community and my community council, and I'll go out

> and walk the streets and, you know, I'll sound
> out people about what they think about cer-
> tain services and that and, you know, I'll try
> and get as close a feeling as I can but ... and
> I think that's all anybody could really do and
> nobody can represent the whole of [this area].

However, this extra consideration of a public role did not in most cases
translate into a change in reported behaviour, and overall there were
remarkable similarities in perspective between elected members and
their appointed colleagues.

Elected Non-exec 6:   I've managed to really deal with that role quite
well and encourage people if they do contact
me or meet me in the street, to really email me
what their concerns or what the story is and then
I email it, you know, to the right person and
that's been working really well, you know, so I'll
not ... I'm no' scared of that role at all because
really what I'm doing is acting as a conduit to put
these things in the hands of wherever it is they
should be.

A significant number of members were elected without anything recognisable as campaigning. For these members, many of whom had a
medical background and had a clear sense of what was 'for the best',
it was possible to understand their role as protecting or advocating for
the greater good of the population without proactively engaging with
them:

Elected Non-exec 21:   I suppose I am [a public representative], but it's
not something that I wake up in the middle of
the night concerning myself about. I'm a member of the Health Board, which is something
I've had wanted to be for quite a long time and
it's worked out in this particular way. I'm more
than happy to help members of the public, to
articulate what they have to say or think, as best
I can, yes, but thus far there haven't been too
many episodes of them coming to me.

The broad (although certainly not total) consensus on this was likely influenced by extensive debates in each Board about the possibility of elected non-executives holding 'surgeries' (in the style of an MP or local councillor) whereby members of the public could come along and discuss their views on local services. This debate went to the heart of whether being an elected member required an ongoing and distinctive approach to the public, or whether the moment of accountability existed simply at the ballot box.

Elected Non-exec 17: I don't have a constituency as such because I don't represent any particular group, you know, the idea of having a surgery where people come along and telling me what's wrong, I mean that would be totally alien for me because I don't regard myself as having that sort of lynch group, and I'm more looking at it more from the sort of general overall benefit with essentially a medical overview.

Elected Non-exec 9: The people elected the non-execs members to do the job for the health of the people. My manifesto was clear, I didn't say I was going to set up surgeries, I told people what I was bringing to the table and they voted on whether they thought I had the skills or not to do the job.

Elected Non-exec 8: No I don't see myself as a public representative, I think the mechanism by which I got on the Board is neither here nor there and I think that's how the government sees it as well, so it was just a mechanism to get people on the Board and then once I was on the Board I just feel that 'this is a job'.

Holding onto this pragmatic sense of one's own legitimacy – 'this is a job' – resolved a number of dilemmas for newly elected members. The absence of active campaigning during the election process was a source of pride to many elected members, meaning that there was something innate about them which convinced and persuaded voters. This was particularly the case where candidate statements had essentially consisted of a brief biography. However, it also meant that a fair number of members were surprised (even in some cases perplexed) to have been successful, and lacked a 'manifesto' to move forwards with. Again, the belief that it was their innate abilities or experience which had earned them their seat, and not a commitment to make specific changes, or even to stay connected to electors, was reassuring, and fitted comfortably with existing Board practice.

Elected Non-exec 13:   Yes, yes, otherwise how, why was I elected with my background, out of the 60-odd candidates how did the populace decide and somewhere in their minds ... all right I might be being very naïve, but part of the reason I would have thought was I had been elected was my previous experience.

In sum, the ostensibly dramatic shift from ministerial appointments to direct public elections did not yield correspondingly dramatic shifts in Board member understandings of their roles within the first two years of the pilot. While it is possible that a slower shift would take place, there is also some evidence that 'business as usual' is more likely to win out over time, given that the one or two 'maverick' elected members had either adopted a more conventional approach or resigned their Board membership within the first two years. In this sense, the radical potential of elections created a window of opportunity for change, to which existing norms of Board membership proved resilient. This study demonstrated that the introduction of direct elections did not transform how Scottish NHS Board members understood their own legitimacy and relationship to the public. However, it did reveal a diversity of perspective among both existing appointed members, and newly elected members. Simply, introducing representative democracy into the institutional structures of (s)election is not the determining factor for these personal and interpersonal orientations.

Within the professional/representative Board paradox outlined by Cornforth (2005), it is assumed that the 'professional' skills required by Board members in the stewardship or principal–agent model are a matter for technical appraisal. Thus the performance of Board members can be measured against the extent to which they held managers to pre-defined performance goals. A representative Board is either understood as performing well when it is 'innately' representative in the

weak democratic understanding of having been chosen in an appro-
priately run election, or in the more thoroughgoing understanding of
democracy when it develops a responsive and accountable relationship
with the public. Interviews with appointed or elected Board members
complicate the clean binary distinction of the theoretical 'paradox'
between a representative and a professional Board. Some appointed
members understood their legitimacy as about technically holding
managers to account using centrally defined targets as a yardstick, but
others still understood doing a 'good' job as about holding onto a personal vision of the public good, and guiding the organisation towards
that. Likewise, while a few elected members traced their legitimacy to
the voting public, and felt that their ongoing relationship with that
public was critical to their legitimacy, others understood the process
of election as akin to a job interview – a hurdle to be overcome and
then forgotten. Within both models of Board membership, individuals
developed personal understandings of their roles, drawing on a wide
range of justifications from sources as diverse as policy documents,
ministerial speeches, guidance given in their training and induction,
or conversations with neighbours and acquaintances in their front
gardens.

Representative democracy and citizen participation in health

As a mode of participation, the extension of representative democracy
into the governance of healthcare organisations is something of an
oddity. In this mode, citizen participation is invited, certainly, but
invited *by* central government *into* the management of healthcare
organisations. Often the organisations which are forced to open up
to elected citizens have not chosen, and would not choose, this mode
of participation. Instead of requiring healthcare organisations to seek
out and listen to their publics, the tools of representative democracy
demand that the public actually choose who runs those organisations.
Ostensibly this is the 'strongest' policy tool for participation available.
And yet, low turnout in standalone elections, and even more so, the
overwhelmingly cautious, collaborative approach of those elected,
means that in practice, this mode seems unlikely to transform the way
that organisations relate to their publics. What is notable from the two
Scottish examples discussed above is that the characteristics we asso-
ciate with elected (party) political arenas – contestation, bargaining,

public visibility – sit uncomfortably within the existing organisational culture of Scottish healthcare organisations. While enhanced public participation within and control of publicly funded organisations is a goal with which few will argue, discomfort and disillusionment with much of contemporary political practice makes the extension of representative democratic structures into health systems an awkward route to achieving it.

6
Fighting the System: Citizen Participation as Protest

In Chapters 6 and 7 we turn from invited modes of action in health systems – committee work, outreach projects, and the creation of new links to representative democracy – to two uninvited, even actively discouraged, modes of public action. This chapter explores public protest and campaigns within health systems, and the next considers the ways in which private tactics of service use can be understood as public action. Public protests in health systems are an example of 'contentious politics', which Tilly and Tarrow (2006, p. 4) define with the following characteristics: the making of claims by one actor; collective action ('coordinating efforts on behalf of shared interests or programs'); and politics (interactions 'with agents of governments, either dealing with them directly or engaging in activities bearing on governmental rights, regulations and interests'). The contentious, oppositional orientation of public protests about the decisions of healthcare organisations explains, I argue, why they are rarely considered within academic or policy discussions of citizen participation in health.

In this chapter, seeking the uninvited contentious public politics outlined above, I concentrate on local grassroots campaigns against hospital closure as an instance of public action which (a) generally targets the decisions of health system administration rather than national policy; (b) springs from opposition to, and involves fundamental challenges to, health system decision-making; and (c) has a spatially concentrated and yet inclusive constituency, with the potential to include publics not currently using health services or experiencing any ill health. At a remove from such local, service-oriented protests, there is a rich literature on the campaigning activities of what are variously described as patients' organisations (Rabeharisoa et al., 2014), health social movements (Brown and Zavestoski, 2004), and health consumer groups (Allsop et al., 2004).

However, the work of many large disease-based patients' organisations has become less politicised and change-oriented in recent decades (King, 2004; O'Donovan et al., 2013). While there are still, internationally, some genuine 'outsider' campaigns which question the medical establishment (for example Aronowitz, 2012; Auwaerter et al., 2011), many more patients' organisations are now welcome partners in health system governance, enthusiastically consulted (Jones et al., 2004) and even in some cases acting as contractors, providing services for healthcare organisations. Allsop et al. (2004) distinguish health consumer groups from protest groups partly on the basis that protest groups are more likely to be critical of the medical establishment.

This chapter begins by considering the international literature on public responses to hospital closure, categorising the different tactics reported when publics seek to oppose decisions. It then describes the recent history of hospital closures in Scotland, and presents data from individuals involved in specific campaigns against closure. I argue that, by questioning both the evidence base of healthcare decision-making and the legitimacy of existing decision-makers, hospital closure protests are an example of profoundly challenging public action. Their omission from contemporary discourses of participation in healthcare reveals some of the problematic biases therein.

Hospital closure protests in international context

Proposals to close hospitals are among the most politicised decisions in healthcare, sitting at the intersection of three major contemporary trends: disinvestment, evidence-based policy, and citizen participation. Internationally, rapid and expensive developments in medical technology, increased specialisation, and shifting demographic trends have forced a rethink of traditional models of healthcare in advanced industrialised societies. Technology-dependent secondary care is increasingly being centralised in cities and large towns, while more routine care is being dispersed to small community health centres. This, it has been argued, creates a surplus of smaller, local hospitals (such as traditional district general hospitals (Pollitt, 2008)). Difficult disinvestment decisions have also been increasingly common in the aftermath of the 2008 financial crisis (Gerdvilaite and Nachtnebel, 2011; Ham, 2009). However, hospital closures are often unpopular with local populations, bringing pressures for evidence-based decisions and cost curtailment into conflict with demands for the public to have a say over the shape of local services.

It is telling that the process of closure is often referred to euphemistically as 'service redesign'. Academic literature on hospital closures tends to assume a scenario of public resistance to either the irresistible march forward of medical progress into centralised units or the pragmatic, budget-cutting closure of facilities in recognition of contemporary fiscal realities. Multiple studies emphasise the emotional (sometimes presented as irrational) attachment which publics can display to hospitals (Barnett and Barnett, 2003; Fontana, 1988; Haas et al., 2001; Lepnurm and Lepnurm, 2001; Reda, 1996). One New Zealand study states that 'large sections of the population had a nostalgic affinity for the "hospital on the hill", however antiquated, inefficient, inaccessible or uncomfortable' (Barnett and Barnett, 2003, p. 66). This resonates with the language often used to describe public protest: 'a storm'; 'an upsurge'; 'an outpouring'. A more sympathetic exploration of this attachment is offered by studies which emphasise the symbolic role that hospitals can play within communities as a manifestation of a locality (Brown, 2003; Gifford and Mullner, 1988; James, 1999; Moon and Brown, 2001) and/or of the wider health system or welfare state (Brown, 2003; Moon and Brown, 2001). This research seeks to understand and explain the 'irrational' way in which publics cling to institutions which have been deemed clinically ineffective or even dangerous.

However, there is remarkably little empirical data on public attitudes and protests to hospital closure. Reviewing the international literature in search of studies which are explicitly interested in public or community responses to proposed hospital closures initially yields a high number of hits (including studies from the UK, USA, Canada, New Zealand, Australia, and Sweden), but on filtering by abstract, it becomes clear that the public is more often an imagined than a researched actor within the contextual narratives of studies. One example is Moon and Brown's study of resistance to a proposed closure of St Bartholomew's Hospital in London, in which he describes one discourse as emanating from a 'public' standpoint, and yet illustrates it only with quotes from newspapers and elected politicians, stating elsewhere that 'The discourses that we examine were largely produced and articulated from within the hospital itself or from the media' (Moon and Brown, 2001, p. 47). One Canadian study, the methodology of which reports no research with members of the public, repeatedly offers definitive statements about public opinion and motivations, commending the government for sticking to a 'rational' decision-making process despite the lure of public emotions (Lepnurm and Lepnurm, 2001).

Where researchers have actually conducted empirical research with members of the public, they report campaigners engaging both in invited consultation activities (of the sort discussed in Chapters 3 and 4) and in a series of uninvited activities, or tactics. Invited activities, in many of these studies, involve more oppositional dynamics than are commonly described in participatory activities. Carefully planned public meetings 'go wrong', as when Abelson's Canadian study describes 'Confrontational public meetings, pitting the community on one side against decision-makers on the other, were held to discuss the options and the community responded angrily and vociferously' (Abelson, 2001, p. 787). While invited, the 'unruly publics' (Felt and Fochler, 2008) within these consultations often surprise decision-makers by responding to invitations angrily, or simply by organising themselves in ways unexpected by authorities. Abelson (2001) reports the classic political tactic of arranging transportation to get supporters to meetings in numbers. Dent's study in an English health authority reports a hospital manager (resistant to proposed closure) suggesting that they 'fill the hall with supporters and have people outside "pissed off" and chanting', while a trade union representative arranged buses to transport supporters (Dent, 2003, p. 121).

Protests become analytically distinct from oppositional responses to invitations to participate, when studies describe a range of uninvited actions. In Figure 6.1 I group these uninvited actions into three categories of tactics. These categories draw on Tilly and Tarrow's (2006, p. 14) discussion of political participation in Germany, which differentiates 'appeals' and 'procedural' actions from 'demonstrative', 'confrontational', and finally 'violent' acts, demonstrating that 'the mix of conventional, confrontational, and violent activities changed dramatically' over a period of 40 years. My categorisation reflects the more measured nature of reported tactics in the literature on hospital closure protests. Firstly, I describe a series of 'procedural' tactics, where publics respond in ways which, while outwith the scope of merely responding to invited opportunities for consultation, are broadly respectful of (and therefore support and reinforce) the official process of decision-making, and acknowledge the legitimacy of those in authority by appealing directly to them. I place petitions, and legal challenges within this category. Similarly, some studies describe a process whereby opponents of closure engage with the (variably 'evidence-based') arguments for closure in an attempt to demonstrate where they are mistaken (Oborn, 2008; Ruane, 2011).

A middle category of 'confrontational' tactics takes on the legitimacy of the decision-making process, challenging it from the outside. Two of

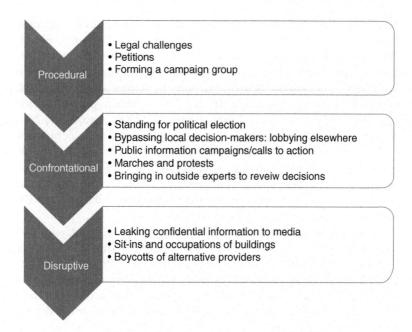

Figure 6.1 Three categories of tactics in hospital closure protests

the most frequently discussed confrontational tactics are marches and protests (Barnett and Barnett, 2003; Brown, 2003; Fulop et al., 2012; Haas et al., 2001; Kirouac-Fram, 2010; Oborn, 2008; Taghizadeh and Lindbom, 2014) and 'going the political route' (Fontana, 1988). Brown (2003) describes the symbolic power of a march of an estimated 12,000 people, led by a horse-drawn hearse, to protest the proposed closure of an English hospital. However, Barnett and Barnett's (2003) New Zealand study, noted that both marches and protest meetings had little impact on actual decision-making, functioning instead, they argue, to relieve stress and direct anger at decision-makers. Whether effective in altering outcomes or not, I include protest marches within confrontational tactics because they are a show of strength that spills outside the prescribed venues of the formal consultation process. They come from the classic political 'repertoires of contention' (Della Porta, 2013) that Tilly (1986) traces back to the French Revolution.

Multiple studies of different health systems discuss the confrontational option of 'taking a political stance' or 'going the political route'. This is often described as a distinct 'step up' phase, after initial procedural tactics fail. This includes tactics such as lobbying 'over the heads' of existing decision-makers and even standing as protest candidates for election. Because it is relatively rare for healthcare organisations to be run by elected officials (Stewart et al., 2015), these candidates tend to pursue higher office, again undermining the decision-making process which has failed to deliver the desired outcome. In Sweden, Lindbom (2014) discussed the development of political parties seeking to protest hospital department closures. Oborn (2008) and Brown (2003) research the 2001 election of a protest candidate as Member of Parliament in Kidderminster, England. A similar, if less newsworthy, approach is to develop realpolitik-esque strategies, such as one American study which described campaigners (led by the hospital board) strategically forging links with an Olympic training centre to get local business interests 'on side' and strengthen the case for retention of acute facilities (Fontana, 1988).

A final category of tactics are disruptive. They seek to actively challenge and disrupt the day-to-day life of the organisation in question, and may skirt the boundaries of legal action. These are far rarer within the international literature on hospital closure protests. Several examples come from one study, Kirouac-Fram's (2010) wide-ranging historical description of opposition to the proposed closure of an urban general hospital in St Louis, USA, in the 1970s and 80s, which had a strong history of serving the city's black population. This protest incorporated sit-ins and occupations (prompting arrests). This physical occupation of threatened spaces is, again, a classic element of the protest repertoire, and a strong symbolic statement as well as a practical disruption of everyday life. Likewise, but relying instead on market-based tactics of 'exit' (Hirschman, 1970), both Kirouac-Fram's US study and Fraser's aborted Australian study report boycotting (whether formally organised or spontaneous) of 'competing' health facilities in a bid to defend the threatened hospital (Fraser, 2004; Kirouac-Fram, 2010). Again, this evades engagement with the formal decision-making process around the closure, and instead disrupts the everyday life of the organisation. This disruption constitutes, in Tilly and Tarrow's (2006) framework, a stronger statement than contentious or procedural acts.

The case of protests against hospital closure in Scotland

In the decade between 2004 and 2014, Scottish Health Boards brought forward 14 proposals to close a total of 26 hospitals as part of 'major service changes'. (This figure was calculated by supplementing proposals which were deemed by the Scottish government to constitute 'major service change' with an analysis of proposals which garnered regional or national newspaper coverage (from *The Herald, The Scotsman, Scotland on Sunday,* and the *Press & Journal*).) The eventual outcome of these proposals (as at spring 2015) was that the closure of 16 hospitals had been agreed. It is noticeable that some hospitals are subject to repeated proposals for closure: these figures include in both the 'retained' and 'closed' columns the proposed closure of three birthing units in Grampian, proposed in 2006 and rejected by the Minister, but then again proposed, and this time successfully closed, in 2012. Since another five 'saved' hospitals were part of a single proposal, only four out of 14 proposals containing hospital closures have been successfully opposed.

The NHS in Scotland has been subject to the same clinical and financial pressures discussed above in an international context, pushing hospital closures up the political agenda. The Scottish context is additionally characterised by a small but significantly dispersed remote and rural population comprising just under a fifth of the total population, and growing faster than the population elsewhere in the country (Scottish Government, 2012). While the definition of the rural population differs internationally, this proportion is similar to Canada's assessment of its rural population (Statistics Canada, 2011), and higher than that in Australia or New Zealand (Baxter et al., 2011; Statistics New Zealand, n.d.). It is widely acknowledged that rural healthcare 'is much more than simply the practice of health in another location' (Bourke et al., 2012, p. 502) and that geographic isolation, in combination with other specifics of a rural context, necessitates distinct models of healthcare provision (Farmer et al., 2007). It has particular consequences for questions of service centralisation (Mungall, 2004).

Since devolution, controversial decisions about hospital closures have been a prevalent feature of both local health politics and the national agenda. Thomson et al. (2008) highlight a 2003 proposal to close two Glasgow hospitals as prompting the escalation of local disagreements to the national stage, including a no-confidence motion in then Health Minister Malcolm Chisholm and the formation of a nationwide campaign to target the parliamentary seats of representatives seen as 'uncaring' about the plight of local hospitals. In 2004, Malcolm Chisholm appointed Professor David Kerr to lead a group of experts to consider 'the future shape of the NHS in Scotland', and by the time the National Framework Advisory Group reported in 2005, Chisholm had been replaced as Health Minister by Andy Kerr. The 'Kerr report' as it is widely known, presented substantial change as inevitable (despite acknowledging that the 'health debate' had 'touched many a raw nerve'), stating that 'it should be obvious to all that the status quo definitely cannot be an option' (National Framework Advisory Group, 2005, p. 2). This change was to involve greater collaboration between services, and entailed the recommendation to 'Concentrate specialised or complex care on fewer sites to secure clinical benefit or manage clinical risk' (National Framework Advisory Group, 2005, p. 6). The government's response, Delivering for Health (as discussed in Chapter 2) welcomed the report, and endorsed it 'as the basis for NHS Boards to take future decisions on the reconfiguration of specialist health care services' (Scottish Executive, 2005, p. 41).

The importance of hospital closures on political agendas since devolution is reflected in the frequency of change of the guidance to healthcare organisations actually *making* decisions on individual hospitals. Until 2002, decision-makers were to be guided by a circular from 1975 ('Closure and Change of Use of Health Service premises'). However, new 'draft interim' guidance was circulated in 2002 (Consultation and Public Involvement in Service Change), again, still in 'draft' form for comments in 2004 (Informing, Engaging and Consulting the Public in Developing health and Community Care Policies and Services) and then again in 'revised' form in 2010. The convoluted, lengthy nature of this process hints at some of the difficulties national politicians have had in balancing expert advice in favour of service centralisation (and thus closures) with local political realities. 'CEL 4', as the 2010 guidance is known, sets out a process of consultation which Boards are required to follow, including evaluation by the Scottish Health Council and approval from central Government. Repeated shifts in guidance can be seen as policymakers attempting, and struggling, to respond to the emergent politics of this issue.

In the research projects this book is based on, historic and current hospital closures were a recurring and emotive topic for many interviewees across all Health Boards studies. Two particular campaigns stood out. In campaign A, the gradual removal of services from a district general hospital to an urban tertiary hospital sparked fears of a systematic attempt to downgrade and run down the local facility. While the Board consistently denied any intention to close the hospital, a highly energetic 'save the hospital' campaign sprang up, successfully putting forward multiple candidates for local government elections. In campaign B, a major redesign of health services across an entire, predominantly rural Board area included proposals to close multiple small 'cottage hospitals' in towns and villages. A major mobilisation opposed the proposals, intersecting with the 2010 pilot Board elections. The proposals were first delayed and then abandoned, but campaigners persisted in a 'watchdog' role, expressing fears that the Board had a more gradual plan to close the hospitals.

Interviews with individuals who had been closely involved with these two campaigns, and the decision-makers these campaigns had targeted, revealed the depth of feeling that these issues aroused.

Campaigner, campaign B: It was an emotional campaign rather than sort of being with, you know, with policy or, you know, political in that sense, it was being really involved locally in the communities and, you know, just caring about the fact that people's local hospitals might be about to close.

This was matched by the feelings of decision-makers past and present, who had been startled and in some cases distressed by the approach taken by campaigners. One Board member described someone spitting at them as they left a meeting. However, other campaigners emphasised the practical bases of their opposition to proposed closures:

Campaigner, campaign A: I always use this example, that the poor old pensioners in [village name] who gets a letter from a God, namely a consultant, saying you have to be in the [centralised hospital] at half past eight for an assessment, and she cannot get there. So in not thinking it through, no officer of the board or department has actually sat down and thought 'there's no bus service in [village name]'. And the best way to do this is a half 10, 11 o'clock appointment, which they now do, but only when it's pointed out to them.

Campaigners described the frustration of trying to engage with official consultation processes:

Campaigner, campaign B: I think I and other campaigners were hopeful that we could really get somewhere within the system, but then very quickly it became clear that that wasn't going to be easy, first of all I suppose that it wasn't going to be easy and then that it really … that we were coming up against a brick wall.

Campaigner, campaign A: ... the frustration really of not knowing why things are happening. And at the same time as not knowing why things are happening, when you ask the question, not getting a clear and concise answer.

In both cases, the decision-making process had eroded the already precarious trust between publics opposed to closure and the Health Boards making decisions.

Campaigner, campaign A: ... a consultation group was set up. But it became a talking shop, so the [campaign] part was a splinter group ... we felt that at the time simply no one was listening.

Public meetings were described as angry and well-attended (in some cases to the surprise of organisers). As remarked by several of the councillors in Chapter 5, public opposition was an uncomfortable and new experience for some Health Board members.

Campaigners resorted to oppositional tactics (as discussed below), but also built ongoing groups, which outlasted any specific proposal threatening a specific facility. Campaign A had been running for years, prompted initially not by closure but by the top-down decision to centralise a major specialism away from one hospital. Campaign B, a more recent grouping, intended to continue beyond the time limits of the then consultation process. Campaigners stressed their suspicions that Boards would close 'saved' hospitals 'by the back door' by gradually reducing bed numbers or service availability:

Campaigner, campaign B: ... that's why we're forming this group, it's partly to be a watchdog, you know, we want to keep an eye cause we don't trust them ... you know, what's going on behind the scenes, if they're running down the beds and so on.

That campaigns operated on their own timescales, refusing to 'stand down' when particular proposals were formally decided upon, one way or another, can be understood as a challenge to the legitimacy and transparency of the decision-making process.

Other aspects of the tactics chosen by campaigners resonate with the international literature discussed above. Public marches and protests of the classical repertoire (Della Porta, 2013; Tilly and Tarrow, 2006), were less prominent in these two campaigns. Instead, they had, echoing some of the discourse-defining actions Moon and Brown (2001) describe, sought to take a considered, 'expert' position. Letters to local press featured prominently. Campaign B had fundraised to commission an external expert to undertake a feasibility study of the retention of the threatened facilities:

Campaigner, campaign B: … if we can get the funding to get a formal academic study by experts then you know that's a very objective sort of evaluation. I find it … I found out that it's better off having an objective independent evaluation.

Working in partnership with other local groups, notably community councils, was mentioned by both campaigns. Campaign B had also sought support and advice from campaigners in other areas of the UK. Both campaigns had also gone 'over the head' of the decision-making process by standing candidates for election in a number of different contests, often successfully. This was rarely understood as seeking to gain a seat at the decision-making table, but to gain an alternative vantage point from which to promote the cause:

Campaigner, campaign A: So the original plan or strategy really was to be elected as a councillor and nip away at other political parties' heels in order to get them to accept a healthcare agenda.

Throughout these narratives, the campaigners described a form of contentious politics that challenged both the legitimacy of existing health service decision-making in Scotland, and the evidence which is mobilised within that decision-making process. These challenges were rarely characterised by emotive outbursts, with the exception of the overspilling of frustrations at officially organised consultative meetings. Instead, campaigners took a more orderly route to contest decisions by seeking positions *within* the system, but *above* the levels of local health service governance.

Protests as a mode of citizen participation in health

Particularly given the current context of financial pressures in health systems, it is critical to understand instances where proactive public mobilisations escalate issues from the administrative or managerial contexts in which decisions are made into the public realm. This chapter has drawn on sociological and political science accounts of 'contentious' politics to explore protests as a mode of engagement between publics and their health systems. The example of opposition to hospital closures juxtaposes dominant 'expert' discourses of clinical and technological progress to perceived emotional and irrational commitment of local publics to the physical presence of hospitals in their communities. In exploring the tactics described in international studies of hospital closure protests, and in the narratives of individuals who have protested against closures in the Scottish NHS, it becomes clear that protest is a mode which straddles invited and uninvited action. Often, protestors mobilise within the parameters of an invited consultation process, although they may draw on 'repertoires of contention' (Della Porta, 2013) to respond to invitations with unexpected shows of force, in terms of both numbers of supporters and strength of feeling. However, invited consultation processes are often perceived as 'dead ends': 'public involvement in a formal NHS consultation exercise is unlikely to have much influence on NHS decision-making' (Ruane, 2011, p. 145). Highly oppositional, contentious, and disruptive tactics (such as well-attended protest marches) may be attention-grabbing, and more procedural tactics such as active engagement with the evidence base for a given closure might capitalise on the authority and legitimacy of 'expert' opinion. A tentative conclusion from the cases explored so far is that going 'the political route' (bypassing local decision-makers in favour of central government elected politicians) is the most frequently successful tactic available to protestors (Ruane 2011).

An account of citizen participation in health systems which limits itself to invited action will thus miss both some of the most resourceful examples of collective public action, but also some of the most 'successful'. (Where success is defined as having a demonstrable impact on local healthcare). Seeking to isolate a particular 'successful' tactic within this mode does not, however, suggest that they are discreet and independent tools that can be lifted neatly from a repertoire. Rather, the emergence, development, and forging of a coalition of actors into a protest is likely to move across categories of action, from returning orderly consultation responses to waving placards and appealing to the self-interest of elected politicians. In so doing, the limitations of our existing academic typologies of citizen participation are exposed. The next chapter follows this line of enquiry further, exploring what happens when an oppositional orientation reveals itself in individual, privatised actions.

7
Playing the System: Citizen Participation as Subversive Service Use

In this chapter we move from the dramatic mode of protests within health systems to an alternative uninvited mode of action. By contrast to its uninvited sibling, this mode is so quiet as to be nearly inaudible, and sits at the very boundary of public and private action in health systems. As such, it provides a particularly puzzling challenge both to policies for participation in health systems and to the existing conceptual structures by which we usually analyse them.

My interest in what I term subversive service use arose from researching a specific group of non-participants within health systems: young adults who engage with neither the invited opportunities that systems create nor the uninvited 'uprisings' of participation which take place within their communities. Young adults – 18–25-year-olds, sometimes referred to as 'emerging adults' (Arnett, 2004) – are an illuminating group of service users to focus on for two reasons. Firstly, their patterns of service use are distinctive, and pose challenges for conventional models of voice and choice. Furlong and Cartmel (2007) discuss youth and adolescence as a time of peak physical health, following childhood vulnerability to congenital and infectious diseases and before the degenerative diseases which are more common in adulthood. Youth is, however, a period of different types of risk, with accidental injury, poisoning, self-harm, and sexual ill-health the most prevalent health problems (Blum and Nelson-Mmari, 2004). The frequency of self-reported mental health problems among young people has grown significantly (Furlong and Cartmel, 2007). Lightfoot and Sloper (2006) point out that most public and patient involvement activity aimed at young people in the English NHS is about health promotion, not services. Accordingly, in young adults' interactions with the NHS their role is rarely that of a straightforward victim of chance. Their health problems may be seen

101

by professionals or society more widely as consequences of their own (intentional or otherwise) actions, or of health issues which remain stigmatised and poorly diagnosed.

Recent generations of young adults are also frequently understood to be less, or differently, politically and civically engaged than other age groups (Furlong and Cartmel, 2007). The gap in electoral turnout rates between the old and the young continues to increase with generations (Russell, 2007, p. 23). However, a significant number of scholars argue that political participation has not diminished, but changed (Dalton, 2008; Norris, 2002; Pattie et al., 2004): 'Political energies have diversified and flowed through alternative tributaries, rather than simply ebbing away' (Norris, 2002, p. 5). Studies of these alternative tributaries are testing the boundaries of definitions of politics, either by moving away from action towards stated views, or by moving away from a social change orientation to focus on lived experience. Marsh et al. (2007), drawing on their qualitative study of youth participation in the UK, argue that young people remain articulate and knowledgeable, and that a lack of formal engagement with politics is a response to their limited efficacy. In a similar vein, researchers have looked away from attempts to change structures towards lived politics. Riley et al. (2010) explore 'neo-tribes' within electronic dance music culture as a 'facet of politics'. Skelton and Valentine (2003) explore the way in which young D/deaf people use British Sign Language as a (political) act of resistance.

The counterpart of a tendency to dismiss participants as 'the usual suspects' is a developing fetishisation of the non-participant. Some of the 'outreach' efforts to reach the elusive 'ordinary citizen' (Martin, 2008b) were explored in Chapter 4. The ill-defined basis of claims to representation which are demanded from, or foisted upon, participants link intrinsically to some notion of a wider 'out-there' public. This entity is sometimes assumed to be singular, as in the case of appeals to 'the' public interest, and sometimes to be multiple, neatly composed of 'communities' or 'groups' who can be identified and engaged in order to satisfy equality or diversity requirements. Where particular groups have proved hard to assemble, the response of commentators has tended to emphasise either apathy or alienation. Both of these diagnoses assume inactivity, and both fail to interrogate whether non-participants might be acting within the health system in some other relevant way, while remaining absent from the conventional spaces of participation. In the next section I recount the ways in which my approach to researching participation in health was challenged and ultimately altered by studying non-participant young adults.

Researching non-participants in the Scottish NHS

My interviews with young adults sat apart from the purposive sampling and snowballing of key informant interviewees which characterised the rest of the data discussed in this book. Purposive sampling was used to select two primary care practices in Rivermouth. A sample of around 200 18–25-year-old patients was created by staff at each practice and a recruitment pack was sent out. Interviewees were paid for their time (with a £10 supermarket voucher), with interviews taking place in winter 2009/2010 in the interviewees' homes and in one case in their workplace. Table 7.1 sets out some characteristics of my interviewees.

This table demonstrates some of the challenges with this sample, including its small size and gender composition. While the total number of interviewees in this section of the research is low, the recruitment was designed to, and succeeded in, reaching young people who cannot be easily recruited through the conventional routes of educational establishments or youth groups (see, for example, Curtis et al., 2004; Marsh et al., 2007). That my invitation to be paid in return for an interview about public involvement was unappealing to the overwhelming majority of the 400 young adults approached suggests a disconnect between the empowering 'opportunity talk' of the policy rhetoric, and how it is received by its target publics.

Once in a room with an interviewee, the difficulty of engaging them in discussion of public involvement policies was a further challenge. None of my interviewees considered themselves experts on health services, even where they had something that they wanted to tell me about their experiences. The topic seemed to risk alienating or intimidating participants. Several interviewees expressed concern that they did not have enough experience, or that they did not have sufficiently

Table 7.1 Characteristics of young adult interviewees

	Number
Men	3
Women	11
In work	7
In full-time education	1
Unemployed	3
On a government training scheme	3
Total interviews	14

'interesting' experiences, to be worth interviewing. Almost any question which sought to place my interviewees in the role of 'empowered citizen' (e.g. 'How happy are you with your experiences of NHS services here?') yielded reluctant, brief answers ('I don't know', 'It's okay'). When probed, answers broadly supported the availability of opportunities for public involvement, but largely as an activity practised by some other group of people. Instead of focusing on my interviewees' absence from the formal mechanisms of public involvement in the NHS, I began to listen to and probe their everyday tales of service use.

Interviewees had varying levels of experience with the NHS. Three reported long-term conditions (asthma, a thyroid problem, and blood clots) and three had worked for the NHS as trainee nurses, healthcare assistants, or administrators. Much of my interviewees' service use was not the life-or-death stuff of grand narratives about the crucial role of health services in our survival, but rather the day-to-day business of keeping bodies and minds ticking over, particularly with regard to their fitness for work. This less fraught relationship with the NHS makes for a fairly abstract commitment to its quality. The resulting 'loyalty' (Hirschman, 1970) was pragmatic, understated, and sometimes unthinking. When asked if there was anything he liked or disliked about his GP practice, David responded:

David: Not really, because when you go to a health centre or whatever, it's just there to, you know, find out what the problem is, get a solution, and just get away. It's nothing, it's not like you have to be attracted to it, it's just, you've got a problem, go to the hospital, go to the health centre, get it sorted out, and get back to living your life.

Visits to their own GP, as well as being in most cases only a couple of times a year, were largely reported as being for mundane issues which resulted in no further action or a course of antibiotics or painkillers. Several interviewees worried, before the tape recorder was switched on or during the interview, that they didn't have enough experience, or interesting enough experience, to be worth speaking to.

The majority of my interviewees were occasional service users who, almost without exception, said they got what they needed from the health services they encountered. 'Aye, that's/they're/it's fine' was by far the most frequent initial response to my questions. Taken together, my interviewees' accounts described mundane, occasional service use.

While this is a common pattern of service use for much of the population, it is one rarely discussed in policy discourse. Much of my interviewees' stories seemed so obvious and familiar to me, as a service user
in the same health system, that it was difficult to attend to as new or
interesting. However, my final interview, with Lisa, a recovering heroin
addict, described a number of troubling experiences with GP practices
which made me reconsider my other interviewees' descriptions. As
something of an extreme case (she had been removed from a practice
list for allegedly missing appointments, had been made to cry by her
most recent GP, and described difficulty getting a recent diagnosis),
hearing Lisa's experiences enabled me to re-evaluate (in some cases
to notice for the first time) similar, if milder, tales, and crucially my
interviewees' responses to them. This is not to detract from the overall satisfaction reported by my interviewees. However, it counters the
assumed passivity of behaviours which, at least from an organisational
perspective, cannot easily be understood as either 'voice' or 'exit'
(Hirschman, 1970).

My interpretation of the accounts I heard from my young adult interviewees is that they firstly *avoided* playing a public role within health
services, and secondly, exercised their agency through *everyday creativity* in interactions with health services. I repeatedly heard about (what
I describe as) tactics used by my interviewees in their interactions with
the NHS. In the context of the NHS, I argue that the moments of agency
my interviewees described, while never engaging with the structures of
'invited participation', are relevant to an understanding of patterns of
citizen participation. Here, I briefly describe the three most commonly
described tactics: avoiding 'bad' doctors, negotiating an acceptable diagnosis, and 'transforming' emergency appointments, before considering
their implications for a policy of public involvement.

Avoiding 'bad' GPs

While it is possible to move GP practice in the Scottish NHS, few of my
interviewees had done so. Most of them had been with their current GP
practice '*always*', since birth or before. There were some quite remarkable tales of 'loyalty' (Hirschman, 1970). Andrew explained that he, his
parents, and his grandparents were all registered with a practice which
was not the closest to his own home, or to his parents' home, but to the
home his mother had grown up in. I asked Laura, who had registered
with a doctor in her university town for one year before moving back

in with her parents, why she had decided to go back to the practice she had been with since birth.

Laura: It wasn't even something I thought twice about. I just, I've never had any negative experiences ... But em, it wasnae really an option. I didn't even think twice about going to find somewhere else, so.

Other interviewees said they had left the area but stayed registered with their previous practice, keeping their parental home as their permanent address. Those who had moved practice reported that they had done so due to leaving town or, in Lisa's case, because she had been removed from a practice list for allegedly missing appointments. Only one of my interviewees said they stayed with a practice because of what I would describe as enthusiasm about the service. At two separate points in the interview Rachel became emotional when discussing the support her GP practice had given her family during a difficult period, and her gratitude to them.

However, while not considering proactively changing GP practice, most interviewees described preferences to see particular GPs within the practice. Highlighting the non-biomedical aspects of patient care (Mol, 2008), almost everyone who expressed a preference justified it with reference to interpersonal factors:

Rachel: She's a friendly doctor, eh? And if you go in and tell her what's wrong wi' you, she em, she'll sit doon and she'll, and she'll try and, cause she's quite young as well so she kindae understands where you're coming fae.

David: I just like to go to that doctor because I like know him ... He's quite cool. Like, not cool, he's no' cool, but he's an all right guy.

Lisa: Silly things, like he sits and he looks at you when he's talking to you and he listens. Where others just sit and type or write.

Where these aspects of the consultation – patience, warmth, familiarity – were absent, they contributed to my interviewees' dislike of other specific GPs in their practices.

Rebecca: It's weird, it's like she's always got that right grumpy look, a' the time. And you go in and a' and you try to speak to her, sometimes she makes you feel a bit, uncomfortable. Because it's like she's no' really got time for you, sort of thing, eh.

David: [on the doctor he avoids] She, she's just quite cold. She
            doesn't really have much, personality.

These varied preferences – smiling, being attentive, understanding,
even 'all right' – point to the emotional labour required of GPs beyond
the medical and administrative aspects of their role. However, Lisa's
reference to 'silly things' here, and other interviewees' use of 'just' to
qualify their preferences, were typical; these preferences seemed deeply
held, but interviewees expressed them cautiously in the interview.
Literature tells us that these factors are not only consistently important
to patients, but are in fact integral to biomedical processeses. Mol, for
example, argues for recognition of how care is 'done', and that 'the
way professionals in day-to-day care practices engage in doctoring and
nursing, in tinkering with and calibrating care, deserves some back-up'
(Mol, 2006, p. 411).

Crucially, everyone who expressed a preference for or against one GP
had some sort of tactic for seeing or avoiding that person. Interviewees
at the practice with the unpopular Dr Jones expressed stronger views
(Lisa: Her I try to avoid at all costs. I dinnae like to see her). Ryan, who
had recently moved to a practice, said he would like to keep seeing the
same doctor, but that 'Aw, I cannae even remember her name!' Most
said they'd ask for an appointment with a named GP, but if it meant
a longer wait, several would take anyone. Several were a little more
proactive:

Rebecca: If I phone, I dinnae want to say 'I dinnae want Dr Jones
              or Dr Stevens'. I'll just say, and if she says 'Dr Jones' then
              I'll just say 'oh no that's no' any good' ... Make an excuse.
              You dinnae want them to make it out eh that you're no'
              actually wanting them, cause then they might say 'oh
              what are you no' wanting them for?' So I just say 'have
              you got another time?'
Interviewer: And would you not like the opportunity to say?
Rebecca: Nuh.
Interviewer: Nah?
Rebecca: Nuh. [Laughs]. I'll just avoid them.

Rebecca was willing to go to some lengths to avoid two doctors she
didn't like, but also to avoid this being registered as any kind of feedback. Dr Jones was mentioned as the doctor they avoid by almost
every patient from that practice (except for Laura, for whom it should

be noted she was the preferred GP, as she was 'to the point'). Megan remarked on this unpopularity:

Interviewer: Are there other doctors that you would prefer to avoid? You don't have to name names or anything.

Megan: Em, probably, if I could. And it is, it's always the doctors that are most available, that's the [laughs], that's the problem. Whenever you phone it's always like 'aye, I can give you them', and you're a bit like 'em, right'.

The lengths to which some of my interviewees would go to avoid unpopular GPs is an interesting example of informal or unsanctioned 'personalisation' (Needham, 2009) by service users. Interviewees were knowledgeable about which GP to see, and had tactics for seeing their preferred doctor. This adds important detail to Leadbetter's account of the 'old script' in paternalistic services: 'phone GP, make appointment, visit surgery' (Leadbetter, 2004, p. 38). This service user activity can be understood as 'subversive' (Prior and Barnes, 2009) of policy; exhibiting service preferences which do not fit into managerial drives for efficiency, and avoiding one's preferences being utilised as constructive feedback. Although there is no way to be certain of this, Megan's comment about the greater availability of unpopular doctors hints at the possibility that within a service provider, the functioning of informal patient choice between individual professionals can create 'sink' GPs, in the same way that we see formal user choice create 'sink schools' or 'sink hospitals' (Le Grand, 1991). Here, an unpopular health professional is less in demand. He or she becomes disproportionately likely to see occasional users and urgent cases, where patient inexperience or distress may create more fraught encounters. This perpetuates a vicious circle for a doctor's reputation.

Transforming 'emergency' appointments

Another example of the way that my interviewees got what they wanted from the NHS was around the use of emergency appointments. However, this was so rooted in common sense knowledge about the process of going to the doctors (my own knowledge, as well as that of my interviewees) that it was less self-evidently 'action' at all. At both the practices I recruited through, the practice information states that a number of appointments are held back each day for emergencies and allocated to patients who phone first thing. One of the practice websites stated:

Urgent appointments: If you have an urgent problem, you will be seen on the day of request if appropriate. Your call will be triaged by our Nurse Practitioner in the first instance. Please try not to ask for an urgent appointment unless you feel this is absolutely necessary.

However, in many of my interviewees' accounts, phoning on the day was presented as the main, 'normal' way of making an appointment.

Rebecca: If you really need an appointment if you phone at eight o'clock, as soon as you get up in the morning, usually they do have some sort of cancellation that day. Might no' always be the doctor you want, but, if you really needed the appointment you could get an appointment, wi' another doctor eh.

Chloe and Megan told me they couldn't call in the morning because of their shift patterns at work, and as a result chose to make appointments in advance. However, calling on the day was still a familiar option.

Megan: I had phoned to make it for like my day off. I generally, I've only been able to get one the day I've wanted it if I phone at like 8 o'clock or something.

Chloe: Mm, it usually is a few weeks. Like unless you phone like every day in the morning. But, usually yeah a few weeks you have to wait.

GP receptionists are increasingly recognised as performing a range of vital emotional and quasi-medical tasks beyond the administrative work they are associated with (Ward and McMurray, 2011). Rachel recounted an anecdote which suggested the tension between practice staff trying to maintain a system of emergency appointments through 'unofficial triage' (Coulter and Elwyn, 2002), and patients trying to use this as the main appointment system.

Rachel: Well I got up at eight that morning and I phoned and I got an appointment, I think it was in the afternoon. Em, it was for Dr Green I got and I went doon at three o' clock eh.

Interviewer: And how do you find the reception?

Rachel: The reception, it, it depends I think. Because sometimes, you could phone in the morning and you wait a long time on getting on the phone. And sometimes, it depends what receptionist's on, they'll maybe ask you why are you wanting an appointment, is it urgent, you know. Like you get a whole list of questions fired at you eh, 'cause when you'd rather just like get your appointment and see the doctors. Ken even if it's just like to ask the doctors a question, you ken, it's, it's no' a case if it's an emergency, if somebody's wanting to see a doctor, they're wanting to see them for a reason eh.

Unhappiness at having receptionists assess one's neediness as a patient was also related to my interviewees' feelings that they were responsible service users. Emma described being far less reluctant to visit the GP as she got older.

Emma: Em, I don't know. It's just before, when you're younger you don't really bother what people think. And then as you get older always think I wonder what they doctors are thinking looking at my notes, saying there's always something wrong wi' her!

For Emma, becoming more responsible as an adult service user equated with using the GP less often. Therefore, when she did decide to phone for an appointment, to be confronted with 'unofficial triage' (Coulter and Elwyn, 2002) was described as unfair.

Negotiating diagnosis

A further area where my interviewees described taking action in the NHS was in negotiating diagnosis, or indeed in deciding to abandon the search for a GP's diagnosis. In contrast to the treatment focus of much health policy discourse, diagnosis constituted the main focus of my interviewees' accounts of health service interaction. It was this stage that interviewees seemed to find most worrying, and it was mostly here that negative experiences occurred. Diagnosis is a crucial process in healthcare interactions, which is imbued with questions of control and knowledge: 'For patients, diagnosis can provide personal, emotional control by way of knowing what is wrong. For medical professionals, diagnosis also provides control by mastering the knowledge of the problem at individual care level' (Brown, 1995, p. 39). Once a diagnosis is reached, individuals can draw on resources of information and support from services and fellow sufferers, and may be reassured about the legitimacy of their worries. However, in the uncertain terrain pre-diagnosis, my interviewees either negotiated a solution (drawing on resources of family knowledge and the internet, and making repeat visits to different individual health professionals until the problem was solved) or chose to opt out of this process (perhaps worrying quietly about an ongoing symptom, or giving it little thought until the moment of our interview). This was an exertion of agency, but it bore little resemblance to assertive service use. This was interpersonal, informal, and frequently unsatisfactory for my interviewees.

Megan's description of the process of trying to be referred on to a clinic for her allergies demonstrated the emotional pressures around diagnosis.

Megan: I, I got sent to an ENT specialist years ago, and he was really really good. And, that's, they [the GP practice] never ever sent me back. I went to see him once, and then they just dealt with the prescription after that. And, again, we just got stuck in a rut with the same things, and they're not helping anymore, so I did say to the doctor 'can I not go back and see them?' And she had just said like 'no, there's no point sending you back, we'll try and do things here', but every time I went back and said 'I don't feel any better', they just kept saying 'well the stuff you're on's the best you get, so you'll just have to keep it'. And it wasn't til I went and seen another doctor, and she was actually really nice, and I said to her, 'could I be referred at all to the hospital', and she actually just admitted 'well yeah, we're at a loss with you, so we're going to have to send you'.

The starting point of confirmation from a specialist is, I would argue, relevant to Megan's persistence in seeking a referral. She described the frustrations of not having her views listened to, but she continued to believe that a return visit to the specialist would be valuable. She spoke emotionally about finally seeing the specialist.

Megan: And I thought thank god. But it took ages of saying before they would actually send me. I don't, I really don't think they wanted to refer me, if they didn't have to .... And it was quite good the first time I seen him, em, when he looked up my

> nose and things he said that you should have come to me
> years ago. And I, I really could of greet [cried] because I, really,
> it wasn't in my mind.

The relief ('I could of greet') of diagnosis, as confirmation of the
legitimacy of her concerns, had for Megan, retrospectively justified her
persistence in speaking up and asking for a referral.

This agential tactic – repeated visits to different GPs until they
reached a diagnosis they found satisfactory – was described by a number
of my interviewees. The process began earlier, reflecting Locker's (1981)
work on causal theorising about problematic symptoms in everyday life.
Wyke concurs that

> It is clear that it is not usually the illness itself that bring patients
> to professionals, but rather their theories as to what the illness is, or
> might be. Thus formal consultations are typically used to confirm
> diagnoses, to help decide between several potential diagnoses, or
> occasionally to ask doctors what the problem is.
>
> (Wyke, 2003, p. 56)

Lisa described the process of getting a diagnosis of gallstones.

Interviewer: So if you had to keep going back, was the diagnosis quite
               complicated then?
Lisa: Well first of all, with the doctor I don't like, she told
               me I was just clinically obese, and you need to lose the
               weight and start eating healthy. Tellt me to give up the
               cigarettes and all the rest of it. The second doctor told me
               I had, eh, ulcers, stomach ulcers, em, and then it wasnae
               until I seen Dr Taylor, and he said 'no, I think it's gall
               bladder'.

Later in the interview, Lisa revealed that she had guessed this eventual
diagnosis earlier in the process:

Lisa: My auntie had a gall bladder out in the June, and this is when my
        pain started coming and causing me nothing but trouble, so my
        auntie was like 'I'm telling you it's gall bladder, it's gallstones', so
        I'm on the computer, googling 'pains in my side' and that's one
        of the things that came up was gallstones, so I read about that
        and I went to the doctors and she said 'no it's not gallstones', this

is when I was told I was obese. 'No it's nothing like that, it's just because you're clinically obese, you're needing to lose weight'.

This combination of information from family and information from the internet is characteristic of the way that most people draw on online health resources. While American research suggests that a Google search is the first step for many people puzzling about a health problem (Fox and Rainie, 2002), it supplements and does not replace existing sources of information (Nettleton and Burrows, 2003). While some commentators point to the transformational effects of online health information ('Medical knowledge is no longer exclusive to the medical school and the medical text; it has "escaped" into the networks of contemporary infoscapes where it can be accessed, assessed and reappropriated' (Nettleton and Burrows, 2003, p. 179)) Lisa displayed considerable reflexivity about this information. Later in the interview she remarked 'I could have been reading anything. Ken? The internet's no' that a fair place'. What Lisa described as making the difference was the agreement of her aunt's suggestion and information she found online (and it is likely her online searching was shaped by her prior knowledge of her aunt's condition).

However, Lisa had used this information to support her persistence in striving for a diagnosis, and not as ammunition for a debate with her GP. When I asked her how she felt about the process of getting this diagnosis, she described using a combination of family knowledge and online medical information not to assertively make her point, but instead as a reason to keep returning to the doctors.

Interviewer: How did you feel about all this?

Lisa: Annoyed. Because I was telling them the symptoms and the symptoms I've got are the symptoms that I'm reading off the computer. At one point I was actually going to print it off and take it to him and say look, there you go, that's what I've got. But, I never done that.

Interviewer: Why not?

Lisa: Cause he agreed to send me for a, well on the third occasion, with Dr Taylor, he was like right, okay, we'll send you for, a scan. An ultrasound. That was that.

Interviewer: Why do you think you decided never to sort of, I don't know, take all the bits of paper and say here, like –

Lisa: I, cause I didnae want, I didnae want to be coming across as being cheeky, and trying to show them to do their job. [laughs]

Lisa described managing the impression the doctors had of her despite being convinced about her diagnosis. The process she described can be understood as pretending to be less knowledgeable than she was to avoid alienating the GP whose formal diagnosis she needed.

Other interviewees recounted tales of diagnosis where they had not been persistent, and which remained unresolved. Emma told me about an evening when her ear started bleeding heavily at a party. Illustrating the galvanising effect of social support, her neighbour persuaded her to go to Accident and Emergency the next morning.

Emma: All [the doctor] done was give me antibiotics and ken I thought, na, am I not getting to go to the ENT clinic? Cause I've got problems with my ears already eh, but it was a coloured doctor eh, ken I couldnae really understand her eh. Ken when you're trying to tell her she's like have you been fighting? And I was like no .... I dinnae ken how it happened. But they just gave us antibiotics and sent us home.

Here, Emma, with past experience of going to the ENT clinic, knew the outcome she wanted. She described communication problems, possibly resulting from her own prejudices ('a coloured doctor') but also aggravated by the doctor's assumptions about Emma ('have you been fighting?'), and her response was to leave, dissatisfied. However, she described still having the physical symptoms, and persisting in her search for a diagnosis.

Interviewer: And so did you go back to your GP to talk through –
Emma: I'm gonnae have to cause I can't stick my ears under the water. And I don't think that's right, eh? My best pal's mum's a nurse eh, and she was like that 'you should be able to stick your ears under water'.

As yet, Emma hadn't pursued the diagnosis but, drawing on accredited knowledge within her social circle, she planned to do so. The marshalling of information from trusted sources was crucial here, as very few of my interviewees talked about feeling confident as an individual to develop an alternative 'story' about their ill health. For example, Rebecca talked about feeling dissatisfied with a recent diagnosis:

Rebecca: I think, to this day, I'm still no' convinced. I mean I'm no' a doctor so I dinnae understand, and the thing that I said to

> my mum is, if it's my spleen, why is it the first time I'm feel-
> ing it? ... It's different if you ken what they're talking about.
> I mean I don't even ken what your spleen is, never mind
> anything else eh? [laughs]

This causal theorising was a common factor of accounts of ill health.
However, it was repeatedly described as happening with family (particularly mothers) and not with health professionals. Asking GPs for
explanations was not mentioned.

The salience of diagnosis is well understood and theorised within
the sociology of health and medicine. Literature tells us that diagnosis is a search for explanation, as well as for treatment (Locker, 1981).
Sociological accounts of the transformation of health information
online and with NHS 24 (the Scottish equivalent of England's NHS
Direct) suggest that patients consult a range of very different sources
in their attempts to make sense of symptoms (Nettleton and Burrows,
2003). However, the patient's role within diagnosis as one manifestation of agency (even control) is only minimally considered in policy-
oriented research, where choice of treatment (as exit) or complaint
about failed diagnoses and treatment (as voice) are more commonly
acknowledged. My interviewees revealed negotiating diagnosis as a
nuanced, subtle business, but one in which self-awareness and agency
were nonetheless present. Despite use of online information and NHS
24, trusted information from friends and family – especially where this
included health professionals – remained central in my interviewees'
decision-making.

Dealing with negative incidents

While interviewees expressed few strong feelings about health services
in general (in answer, for example, to 'How do you find your practice
generally?' or 'How happy would you say you are with the NHS here
generally?'), most of the women had stronger views on particular
incidents where things had gone wrong. (It is important to reiterate
here that the way interviewees were recruited may have increased this
number). There was a clear gender divide, with men having both fewer
interactions with the NHS overall, and reporting very few negative
interactions. Laura recounted an incident from her childhood.

Laura: Em, and that was my own doctor I saw and she was sort of, sort
          of just brushed it off as I'd just knocked it or something but it

was, it was so, like a definite cyst, like you could tell. And when I saw the second doctor, em, it was like a case of me walking in and she was, like she noticed it straight away and said 'that's a cyst' and referred me up to [the hospital] to have it like surgically removed.

Lauren reported a delayed appointment where she was unhappy with the diagnosis and the GP's manner.

Lauren: So I get to the room and I told her that I had been coughin' and spewing up blood again, and that I, my weight kept going up and down and I was down to a size 10 at the time, and she says 'oh, I don't see', I, I don't remember her exact words. Pretty much saying to me no, I don't believe you. And then I says em yeah, and I'm coughing up blood blah blah blah. 'Are you sure about that?' My reply to her was 'well I've been waiting, I'm 35 minutes late for my appointment, I've got to get back to work, I'm not going to be sitting wasting a doctor's time'.

Lisa, a recovering heroin addict who has been 'clean' for some years, became tearful as she described how a new GP responded to her history.

Lisa: As soon as she found out I was a heroin addict, well, ex-heroin addict, she wouldn't touch me. She stood at arm's length and she made me feel so awkward I left the surgery in tears. Because the way she, like she asked me about my past, and I told her, and as soon as I said that it was like a totally different person.

Crucially, none of the negative incidents described had resulted in any formal action being taken by my interviewees. Although Sarah still asserted determinedly that she 'is gonnae sue', most of my interviewees were very clear that they would not complain about their treatment. Even where tales of trouble were far more prominent (particularly for Lisa, Laura, and Sarah), no formal action had been taken.

Lisa: I was actually going to complain, about, the doctor who made me feel terrible. About my past and stuff, I was gonnae complain about her. But, I, I, I never. I don't know why I never, because I was determined and, cause she had me crying and everything. That's hard for me, to cry, something like that I just, normally I just brush it off but she did make me feel that small.

After Lauren's experience she had gone to the reception desk to complain and had been told to write a formal letter to the surgery, but never had.

Interviewer: What would make you send that letter? Like, or what would have made you write the letter with all the details and, because you said you don't have time but –

Lauren: If I had, if I had enough time that's what. I think it was because after a couple of days I thought there's no point if I do that anymore ... and if they had a quick form it would have been right in, there would have been no doubt about it. But, just, sometimes it's no' worth the hassle.

Rebecca and Rachel both said they had chosen not to complain about negative incidents, with Rebecca preferring to 'rant and rave' at her mum. Instead, my interviewees favoured informal, even subversive, strategies (as discussed above) to avoid the offending individual in future.

While the usual explanations focusing on resources of confidence and information to complain are relevant (Allsop and Jones, 2008), I would argue that the limited practical importance of NHS encounters in my interviewees' lives was key to their decision not to 'go formal' with their preferences or complaints. In short, the translation of unhappiness into a more formal type of service knowledge is, I would argue, less likely to take place spontaneously where one's service use is occasional and primarily mundane. My interviewees did not anticipate being frequent visitors to their GP practices in the immediate future, and many of their health needs related to conditions which were short-term or not impinging on their day-to-day lives. Accordingly, I would argue that my interviewees could compartmentalise (or put to the back of their minds) dissatisfaction with their GP practice. This is not to belittle the discomfort of their health issues. Even in cases where an unhappy interaction with the NHS was continuing to impinge on daily life (as in the case of Lauren being unable to put her head under water in the shower, or Megan having time off work because of her allergies), my interviewees displayed remarkable patience. A more frequent or experienced health service user would be confronted more often with awareness of the problem, and perhaps opportunities to articulate it as unacceptable.

Service use as a realm of agency

From the perspective of the heavily normative literature and policy on participation (Clarke, 2013; Moini, 2011), it is tempting to discount my interviewees' reported actions simply as examples of non-participation. But the young adults in my study were not passive in their relationships with health services. By listening to the way that my young adult interviewees talked about using health services, I argue that their 'tactics' can be read as public action in two distinct ways. Firstly, silent inaction in response to an opportunity to engage can be understood as political. Low response rates to my request for interviewees, and the anxious 'I don't knows' of pilot interviews can be seen as part of the same phenomenon as the struggle to get young people particularly, and members of the public generally, to participate in public involvement. Low awareness of these opportunities and confusion about what they are clearly contribute to unwillingness to take part. However, accounts of 'refusal' of policy aims (Prior, 2009, p. 31) and 'withdrawal' from collaborative interventions (Sullivan, 2009, p. 49) illuminate the way that this can be understood as an active behaviour. Hirschman (1970) includes 'separatism' in his modes of exit, which Patterson (2000, p. 689) describes as 'a form of silent discourse that is so deviant and invisible that it embodies implicit critique of the mainstream, coming "close" to a form of voice'. The essential point here is that policies for participation are particularly easy to subvert. Where, for example, refusal to comply with a welfare regime requires a negative action, the inclusive, positive tone of opportunities to participate can be very easily unsettled by individuals simply going about their everyday business. While it is easy to understand this as apathy, it can also be understood as a very profound rejection of the opportunity.

A second approach is to understand use of public services and the opportunities for 'everyday creativity' therein (de Certeau, 1984), as (political) claim-making. This position draws on a tradition of research which investigates the welfare state as a site of politics (Piven and Cloward, 1972), and more recently on Soss's (2000) research with recipients of two types of benefit – a social assistance programme and a social insurance programme – and investigates the citizenship implications of the process of claiming.

> As a mode of political action, welfare claiming is distinguished by the fact that it allows citizens to gain a direct and personalised response from government. Welfare bureaucracies are more accessible than most government institutions and offer citizens more immediate, targeted, and tangible remedies.
>
> (Soss, 2000, p. 59).

It is not customary to understand going to the GP, calling NHS 24, or attending Accident and Emergency as claim-making. However, when my interviewees, most of whom were in relatively good health, spoke about visiting the doctor, it revealed a process of decision-making, including multiple incidents when the problem was eventually deemed too trivial to proceed. Eventually making the telephone call was, like Soss's respondents' accounts of welfare claiming, a decision rooted in social expectations, norms, and advice from friends and family. Attending to this decision-making 'recovers the agency of people who seek to mobilise their government's welfare institutions' (Soss, 2000, p. 59). Particularly in cases where interviewees quietly persisted in seeking care for a medical problem which they had been told was simply a by-product of their lifestyles, this agency is brave and significant. Recognising policy pressures for 'responsible' service use – particularly around 'inappropriate' use of Accident and Emergency, but also present in the Rivermouth system of emergency GP appointments – helps us to appreciate the political dimensions of seeking care through health systems.

Conclusion

Attention to individual experience is more commonly associated with consumerist motivations than with public action. Rethinking participation allows us to draw the everyday tactics of service use described above into our analysis. Acknowledging the significant work that goes into ostensibly straightforward service avoids dismissing the 'silent majority' of citizens who do not actively participate in either invited opportunities for participation or pro-active protests and campaigns, as active agents in their own relationships with their health system.

The occasional 'everyday creativity' (de Certeau et al., 1980) or resistance I discerned within the lives of my young adult interviewees is oppositional in its evasion of responsibility for health service governance. The doctors, nurses and receptionists who form the bulk of their interaction with the NHS are often helpful and occasionally essential to their lives. While describing appreciation when things go well (as they mostly had for most of my interviewees), when the organisation, or individuals within it, falter or fail their reaction is not that of a confident 'co-owner' but that of an anonymous outsider. I argue that my interviewees are describing an orientation to local health services which, instead of embracing the 'partnership and collaboration' which policy aspires to, is more adversarial and critical. As discussed above, these acts are unlikely to have a broader influence because examples of ostensibly poor service from health professionals remain unregistered at an organisational level. I would argue that they are, nonetheless, a problematic omission from current conceptual and policy models of participation.

Acknowledging that there is scope for citizens to subvert and resist policy intentions in these spaces raises further questions. My interviewees' subversion of the rationing of resources (in the form of the emergency appointments system) was largely based on their own convenience. There was no sense in their descriptions of 'going to the doctors' that they acknowledged the collective systemic consequences of their individual decisions, nor that they sought to achieve systemic change by continuing to make appointments in the way that worked best for them. This resonates with Prior and Barnes's (2009, p. 191) argument that we should avoid 'identify[ing] subversion as a heroic, revolutionary or necessarily even conscious act deliberately intended to undermine a particular purpose or outcome of public policy'. Likewise Abu-Lughod (1990) cautions against the 'romanticisation' of resistance, advocating instead careful engagement with the 'analytic dilemmas' that tactics generate. The analytic dilemmas generated by the empirical examples of participation discussed in this, and the preceding chapters, are the subject of our final chapter.

8
Rethinking Citizen Participation in Health Systems

Citizen participation has been high on health policy agendas across the developed world for decades: this alone justifies efforts to understand the policies and practices which have sprung up in response. However, if we also intrinsically care about the project of healthcare as a *public* good, requiring responsiveness to citizens and respect for their agency, then our need for a full understanding of what participation means and does in contemporary health systems becomes even more pressing.

Critical scholars of participation have often explored the way in which facilitators of a participatory activity translate the utterances of the publics they have assembled into flipcharts, then notes, and then reports which are presented to decision-makers as the 'deliverable' outputs of the process. Knowledge is *inscribed*, as Freeman and Sturdy (2014) argue, to render it both stable and easily communicable. This inscription (Escobar, 2014) is an often neglected aspect of the way in which citizen participation sits within broader processes of democratic governance. In Chapter 4 I described one (possibly extreme) instance of this process from within my fieldwork, describing the way in which an outreach worker faithfully documented the sometimes disturbing utterances of participants in an outreach project ('kill the junkies'), but then within the document transposed this into first a set of more acceptable 'views' on local health services and then finally into a set of policy recommendations based (tenuously) upon those views. Anger at other members of the community, ambivalence about health professionals whose roles are simultaneously to serve and to discipline the population they work with, and other analytic misfits thrown up within the participatory process were all excised from the section that would be most likely to be read by decision-makers with power. Thus institutions and the individuals who 'do participation' within them summon a particular imagined public

(Barnes et al., 2007, 2003), but also specify the boundaries of acceptable 'view' or 'experience' to move forward within the process.

In this book, and particularly in this chapter, I propose that scholars of participation in health systems should apply similar critical thinking to their own role in inscribing, and thus shaping what participation in health is. As researchers, we should acknowledge the extent to which we play a similar filtering role to that of the participatory facilitator. Current conceptions of participation in the mainstream health literature are, as I argued in Chapter 1, predicated narrowly upon current policy, and as such they exclude much of the action that publics take within their health systems. The conceptual flex within this book is prompted by a desire to make space within my research for the embodied worries of members of the public, and how individuals act on them. The limits of my understanding of participation were first tested by tacit knowledge about how one interacts with a healthcare organisation to resolve 'troubles' (Schegloff, 2005). Having interpreted this 'uninvited' action as relevant to participation in health, I was confronted by other candidates for inclusion. Why was writing to a local elected politician not within my (implicit) typology (even if, or perhaps especially where, that elected politician has no remit for health)? Why was the campaign group who meet to 'save' their local hospital missing? There might be obvious reasons why these modes of participation are absent from the policy toolbox which I described in Chapter 2, but their omission from broader academic typologies of participation seems curious.

Dorothy E. Smith (2005, p. 24) has written about the sociologist's role in starting from 'within people's actual experience, aiming to explore what lies beyond the scope of an ordinary knowledge of the everyday into the social relations that extend beyond us and catch us up in organisation and determination that we cannot see from where we are'. This book has endeavoured to elaborate not merely the institutional webs in which publics are caught, but the contribution of researchers to maintaining elements of these webs. It has entailed a shift from participation to 'publics and their health systems', and in this chapter I explore the ramifications of that shift further. First I review the modes of engagement elaborated in the preceding five chapters. Then I describe the actual or potential interactions between them, mapping them on three analytic continuums, and suggesting the ways in which they cluster together or contradict. Finally, I discuss the challenges of 'keeping the institution in view', and balancing a desire to acknowledge and report the actions of citizens with a reluctance to turn our critical lens from political-structural factors onto individual behaviour.

Five modes of participation

Having introduced the topic of participation in health in Chapter 1, and the case study of the Scottish NHS in Chapter 2, the empirical chapters of this book described five modes of engagement between publics and their health systems. These modes are depicted in Figure 8.1, clustered into 'invited' and 'uninvited' groups.

In Chapters 3 and 4 I divided 'invited' forms of engagement into two groupings, committee work and outreach work, based on their characteristic features and the assumptions about desirable publics which I argue they embody. Each of these two modes encompasses many techniques and forms which advocates of participatory technologies would doubtless argue are distinct and separate: Warren (2009b, pp. 5–6) lists a selection of these techniques, and estimates that there are 'most probably, nearly one hundred named processes', Smith (2005) offers '57 democratic innovations from around the world'. The preference to label and formalise different participatory techniques (and to defend the boundaries of those labels) relates in part to immersion in the detail of such activities, and partly to a process by which '"experts of community" who claim to hold the expertise on how to create forums that give voice to publics, end up designing, operating and marketing techniques of citizen participation' (Felt and Fochler, 2010, p. 220). Voß (2015) describes this as political participation becoming 'technologized'. However from a citizen's-eye perspective, the shared characteristics within these modes seem more significant than their diversity.

Chapter 3 described committee work, the now somewhat unfashionable, but remarkably obdurate, option of either inviting a small number of citizens to join an existing committee within an organisation, or setting up a standing committee of citizens who then feed in to the decision-making process. Drawing on observation of and interviews

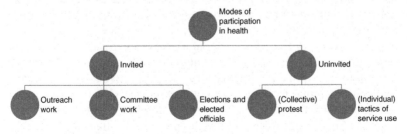

Figure 8.1   Modes of participation in health

with members of such committees in the Scottish NHS, I set out three defining characteristics of this mode: a lack of formal linkage between 'representative' and the wider public; an essentially bureaucratic orientation where practices (reflecting the decision-making processes of the organisation) are largely concerned with agendas, minutes, and action points; and a medium- or long-term level of commitment from participants. Following other academic work (Greer et al., 2014a), I identified committee work as a predominantly 'volunteeristic' mode of engagement, where participants are often concerned to 'help' organisations rather than seek to advance an agenda of change.

Chapter 4 draws together a sweeping range of interactions within 'outreach work'. My empirical data discusses a range of one-off projects run by community development workers and participation professionals in Rivermouth, particularly those with the goal of 'hearing from' or 'involving' young people. Some of these closely resemble small-scale participatory action research projects or deliberative engagements, while others are more akin to opinion polling or focus groups. These are initiated by NHS staff where 'gaps' are noted either at managerial level or by enthusiastic advocates of community development at operational level, and designed (in a somewhat unfortunate metaphor) to 'pick off' defined 'hard-to-reach' groups.

Chapter 5 concentrates on modes of engagement which enlist the techniques and structures of representative democracy into health systems. This includes both strengthening linkages between existing elected politicians and healthcare organisations and creating new processes of formal election to choose new elected representatives. In the first case I drew on data from local authority councillors who sit on Scottish Health Boards, and in the second I discussed a (now discontinued) 2010 pilot of direct elections to choose non-executive members of Health Boards. The key characteristic of the opportunities this mode creates for members of the public is the diversity of action available. Citizens may simply cast a ballot, or they may stand for election themselves or campaign for a preferred candidate. They might, following the election, make contact with those elected representatives to lobby for a particular issue, or to complain about a personal experience. While it is often assumed to be a *stronger* form of democratic control of healthcare organisations, from an individual citizen's perspective it is fraught with difficulties familiar to students of political science. One vote is unlikely to significantly influence the outcome of an election, and one elected representative is (relatively) unlikely to profoundly alter the course of a decision. Altering the means by which decision-makers are chosen may have remarkably little impact if the culture of healthcare organisations does not make a more wholesale shift towards openness to the public, even (or perhaps especially) when unpopular decisions are looming.

Exploring such situations further, Chapter 6 turned to more clearly 'uninvited' modes of engagement available to members of the public: bottom-up campaigns and protests. Taking the illustrative example of opposition to (the often euphemistic term) service reconfiguration, I reflected on the international literature on publics and hospital closure processes, presenting a tri-fold categorisation of the procedural, confrontational, and disruptive public actions which are reported in response to threats to hospitals. I described the way in which local hospital closure protests have shaped and, at times, dominated, national health politics in Scotland since devolution. Finally, I drew on data from activists who mobilised to defend local hospitals put at risk of closure, examining their reasons for taking this (relatively effortful) route to seek influence within their health systems, and the ways in which they reported 'doing' protest.

Finally, Chapter 7 drew in the most unconventional of my five modes of engagement; a range of illustrative uninvited tactics available to individuals in their everyday interactions with health services. What I term 'subversive service use' is not explicitly oppositional in the way that a protest is. It originates from a position of perceived powerlessness within a system, and seeks only to navigate that system in order to meet perceived needs. These included rejecting appointments with unpopular GPs, using emergency appointments for routine concerns, and repeatedly reporting the same symptoms to different GPs until an acceptable diagnosis was reached. This unspoken (or quietly spoken) knowledge about how to 'work the system' without engaging with it can be understood as everyday creativity (de Certeau, 1984; de Certeau et al., 1980). It is not the assertive service use which policy prescribes, nor the activism described in Chapters 5 and 6, but a more personalised, outsider, way of individuals achieving their preferred outcomes.

In setting out this neat typology of modes of engagement I am imposing convenient tidiness on what in reality more closely resembles a muddle of options and possibilities. Citizens may stand for election, to be placed on a committee where they may (or may not) be seen as a representative of the public as they do 'committee work'. Taking part in an invited outreach project can generate opportunities for resistance and subversion, even protest, as a conduit is opened between publics and healthcare organisations. Prolonged resort to subversive service use might drive an individual to engage with the system via a protest or forum. However, in heuristic terms, I argue that specifying and distinguishing modes of participation enriches our understanding of the topic. These modes are not a definitive menu, but rather a starting point from one system, theorised inductively from empirical data. In Chapter 2 I consider the extent to which my empirics are specific to a time (the early 2010s) and place (Scotland). Other modes can be mapped on in interesting and valuable ways. Nonetheless, as this chapter will argue, the five elaborated at length in this monograph clarify, challenge, and extend our understanding of participation in healthcare in fruitful ways.

Interactions

In Chapter 1 I argued that the literature on citizen participation in health has been concerned primarily to support organisations to 'do' participation better. This has entailed (a) a focus on invited opportunities for participation (as uninvited participation is rarely welcome and by definition unsummoned) and (b) an emphasis on evaluating participation along a single continuum, that of the extent to which power is transferred from organisations to publics. This book starts instead from the standpoint of citizens, and presents and explores a range of modes of engagement available to publics. It is my argument that the selection of a particular mode (while likely not a clear-cut decision from a menu of options presented by economists such as Hirschman (1970)) depends on more than an assessment of how likely a given course of action is to yield power or advance an individual's self (or group) interest. Rather, it reflects individually held, and perhaps rarely articulated, knowledge: about the organisation with which one seeks to engage; about one's place (or lack of) within that organisation; and about the communities in which one exists.

Having discussed each of these modes in isolation, this section seeks to map them together onto the notional landscape of a health system, via a series of three conceptual continuums:

- Individual ↔ collective action
- Invited ↔ uninvited action
- Conservative ↔ activist action

The placement of modes along these continuums is not entirely fixed. Any given instance of action within a mode will have some scope for discretion. Sitting on a committee can be done in a more or less activist fashion, for example. However, the modes have strong tendencies in particular directions (see table 8.1).

Table 8.1 Matrix of modes of participation

	Committee work	Outreach	Voting	Protest	Subversive service use
Individual/ Collective	Collective	*undefined*	Individual	*undefined*	Individual
Invited/ Uninvited	Invited	Invited	Invited	Uninvited	Uninvited
Conservative/ Activist	*undefined*	*undefined*	*undefined*	Activist	Conservative

The first continuum specifies the extent to which a mode is individual or collective; whether one acts alone or in concert. Collective action – the coming together of citizens – is often seen as a fundamental feature of citizen participation, which distinguishes it from consumeristic empowerment. However, if we acknowledge the potential discomforts of coming together (Warren, 1996), in particular for people who dislike or are disliked by sections of society, then excluding individually taken action blinds us to how many people influence their health services. Of course, any action can be discussed with others, and all modes are embedded within social contexts. Chapter 7 on subversive service use exemplifies the way that ostensibly individual action is rooted in shared systems of tacit knowledge. However, the moment of action does not require collaboration with other people, and this might be the exact appeal of individual actions such as voting for those who find themselves, by choice or necessity, ill disposed towards or on the fringes of social settings.

The second continuum I propose concerns the initiation of the interaction between public and system; the extent to which action is invited or uninvited. This dimension has been touched on briefly within existing literature on participation and health, but most of the literature takes as its starting point the opportunities created by institutions for the public. Wider political science and development studies literature more consistently mentions the potential for uninvited participation. Sartori (1970) argued that political scientists were routinely confusing 'participation' with 'mobilisation' in the 1970s, and Gaventa (2006) distinguished 'invited spaces' from 'claimed/created spaces'. But perhaps the most thorough development of this generally overlooked distinction is found within accounts of participation in sociotechnical issues. Wynne's (2007) review essay of what he describes as a 'political-conceptual category mistake' repeatedly argues for greater attention and respect to be paid to uninvited participation:

> What difference does it make ... if we recognize that 'public engagement or participation' can be *uninvited*, and not just, as is often taken as a definitive property of 'public participation', *invited*? This very notion of citizens requiring to be invited before they can 'participate', has already sold the pass in its implication that such citizens lack important qualifications to be autonomous public actors, especially ones which would enable them to coordinate and mobilise forms of independent collective meaning, knowledge, judgement and action, whether invited or not.

Indeed, Wynne seems to conclude not only that his fellow STS scholars have a responsibility to challenge the hegemonic focus on invited modes of participation, but that truly democratic practice requires that invited participatory processes should seek to mobilise 'the normal repertoire of spontaneous and independent, uninvited forms of civil participatory action' (Wynne, 2007, p. 107) as an output of the process itself. For my purposes, the invited/uninvited distinction is one of the simplest to apply to the modes of interaction evident within my data. There is a reasonably clear distinction between a space in which the 'rules of the game' are defined by organisational actors, and one in which they are improvised by citizens. Applying this continuum to current understandings of participation in healthcare has the potential to re-politicise a field of practice that too often looks benign and procedural; acknowledging that the 'awkward' publics who insist on exerting their agency in unsolicited ways are 'participating' as much as those who act in invited ways.

Relatedly, the final continuum is, as the undefined cells in Table 8.1 suggest, perhaps the trickiest in which to place modes, particularly for the three 'invited' modes. This is the extent to which action seeks to effect systemic change, as opposed to action which seeks merely to navigate the system as it currently operates. This dimension to some extent correlates with intensity and duration of engagement (reformist tactics often being more 'hit and run' than long-term), and in co-authored work I have described the conservative end of this spectrum as 'volunteeristic' in recognition of this correlation:

> a volunteerist model would suggest that people willing to engage with health care organizations are people who wish to help the

organization on its own terms, without substantially questioning its basic activities or seeking to introduce contentious politics. The idea is to reinforce and support, rather than critique or change it.

(Greer et al., 2014a, p 223)

Applying this continuum to my five modes of participation highlights the scope for self-determination within participatory activities. Both protest and subversive service use can be charted on this continuum: one method defined by challenging the status quo, the other defined by actors simply navigating the system as best they can. However, in all three invited modes of engagement, participants can shape their roles. Chapter 3 demonstrated the way in which a single committee of public representatives contained a mixture of volunteers and activists. The dominant mode of functioning was volunteeristic and supportive of current practice, but activists could carve out space for their agendas within the limits of the forum. Likewise, Chapter 5 argued that newly elected Board members found themselves in a surprisingly volunteeristic setting, but some nonetheless attempted to effect change.

Table 8.1 demonstrates some unexpected associations. The perhaps surprising 'conservative' orientation of much subversive service use is intimately connected to the individualism of the action taken. My interviewees' subversion of the rationing of resources (in the form of the emergency appointments system) was largely based on their own convenience. There was no sense in their descriptions of 'going to the doctors' that they acknowledged the collective systemic consequences of their individual decisions, nor that they sought to achieve systemic change by continuing to make appointments in the way that worked best for them. This resonates with Prior and Barnes's (2009, p. 191) argument that we should avoid 'identify[ing] subversion as a heroic, revolutionary or necessarily even conscious act deliberately intended to undermine a particular purpose or outcome of public policy'. Likewise Abu-Lughod (1990) cautions against the 'romanticisation' of resistance, advocating instead careful engagement with the 'analytic dilemmas' tactics generate. Although uninvited, 'subversive' action can be unfashionably conservative in its effects, unlike the change-oriented challenge of protest.

The *undefined* cells are places where the mode is contestable; where members of the public can choose how to interact with a health system within particular modes. On the individual/collective spectrum, there is scope for citizens to seek out or avoid a collective experience, depending on their preferences. On the conservative/activist spectrum, only protest and subversive service use are intrinsically committed to one or the other: the example of styles of forum membership discussed in Chapter 3 highlights the way in which invited spaces shape, but do not determine, what goes in within them. All three invited modes of engagement can conceivably be used either to support or to seek to change an organisation.

Keeping the institution in view

Having offered an analytic map of the five modes of engagement outlined in this book and identified potential interactions between them, I want in this section to follow the advice of McCoy (2006), a Canadian institutional ethnographer, to 'keep the institution in view'. In her account of the health service interactions of a group of HIV patients, she demonstrates both the challenges and the rewards of working with 'everyday' interview accounts, not merely to understand individual behaviour, but to cast light on the wider social structures (the 'ruling relations') which constrain and shape that behaviour (McCoy, 2006). This offers a way past the analytic dead-end of simply presenting modes of engagement as a benign 'menu' of options from which citizens can freely select.

While my research demonstrates that (as others have noted (de Certeau, 1984; Scott, 1990)) even individuals who appear to have very few resources with which to assert themselves within powerful systems can find ways to exert and express their agency, publics remain profoundly shaped by the experiences through which they come to know those systems. In every mode discussed in this book, healthcare organisations are not merely the detached target for public action, but the context for it. As a more critical literature has developed around what others have described as a 'virtually hegemonic' discourse of public participation (Braun and Schultz, 2010, p. 403), it has been increasingly acknowledged that the design and conduct of invited participatory opportunities does not form an impartial conduit for spontaneous expressions of opinion, but intimately shapes the outputs they yield:

> 'The public' we argue, is never immediately given but inevitably the outcome of processes of naming and framing, staging, selection and priority setting, attribution, interpellation, categorisation and classification. (Braun and Schultz, 2010, p. 404)

The invited spaces discussed in Chapters 3–5 structure the modes of participation played out within them; they assemble particular publics, shape the way that they interact, and translate the outputs into systemically acceptable forms (Mahony et al., 2010). Individuals have, or can usually achieve, agency within these modes, but as the analysis in Chapter 3 suggests, many of them are drawn to these spaces by essentially supportive, rather than change-oriented, goals. Willingness to participate in an invited mode of engagement depends not just upon goals, but on self-knowledge. Likewise, the experiments with inserting representative democracy more firmly into the governance of healthcare organisations which I discussed in Chapter 5 have proven to be highly shaped by the expectations of participants. Even with a 'democratic' mandate to make decisions, citizens look to their organisational context in knowing how to 'do' the mode of engagement they operate within.

By contrast, looking beyond these spaces reveals the complicated journey from individual patient to (public) participant for individuals who are prompted into action by a negative experience, and who understand their relationship to their health system and/or community in particular ways. When it comes to the uninvited modes which I explored in Chapters 6 and 7, the absence of active recruitment by the healthcare organisation only marginally diminishes its influence over how any given individual understands their role and their scope for action within a system. Organisations which 'treat' (or, for that matter, educate, care for or rehabilitate) members of the public send out strong messages about the relationship between individuals and the system within every interaction. Negative interactions with the NHS – those which made my interviewees feel small, or silly, or fat – impeded the development of their sense of legitimacy, leading them to 'pick up messages that their problems are not public but private and of their own making' (Ingram and Schneider, 2007, p. 179). This made it difficult for individuals to understand 'a personal trouble ... as an actionable public issue, a matter of justice' (Pitkin, 1981, pp. 347–348), and therefore to summon the courage to take public action.

Broader literatures from marginalised positions of gender, ethnicity, or social class, describe the risks of 'going public', and the advantages of privacy and silence (Lorde, 2012; Patterson, 2000). Lorde (2012, p. 42) writes that 'the transformation of silence into language and action is an act of self-revelation, and that always seems fraught with danger'. There seems to be something particularly self-revelatory about going public with one's experiences of ill health and health services, as Cornwell's (1984) well-known distinction between private and public accounts of experienced health suggests. Both the articulation of a justice claim and the decision to adopt 'insider tactics' require opening up one's personal

decisions and body for public judgement. Warren (1996, p. 248), reflecting on the gap between easy evocations of a more democratic society
and the likely consequences of it, describes politics as a realm of 'extensive contestability', and an inherently uncomfortable place. Latour
(2005, p. 13) argues that in most cases: 'we don't assemble because
we agree, look alike, feel good, are socially compatible or wish to fuse
together but because we are brought by divisive matters of concern into
some neutral, isolated place in order to come to some sort of provisional
makeshift (dis)agreement'.

Conclusion

Exploring the boundaries of public action in health systems reveals
the existing diversity of modes of citizen participation, and highlights
how narrowly current policy debates conceive of citizen agency. In the
assumptive world of policy, power is held by healthcare organisations,
to be handed over (in prescribed ways and venues) to members of the
public. Debates in health policy between 'choice and voice' (Greener,
2008) direct our attention towards a pre-defined range of acts, and away
from agency more broadly conceived, as governments 'explicitly recog-
nize, and attempt to influence and utilize, the agency of subjects' (Prior
and Barnes, 2011, p. 269). Approaching research with the public from
a policy perspective deems patient choices between competing providers interesting, and patient choices between non-competing providers
invisible (except where patients make 'inappropriate' choices, thus
overburdening emergency care (see, for example Philips et al., 2010)).
However proponents of 'voice' – developing, formalising, and marketing participatory techniques – can be equally blinkered to the myriad of
ways in which 'unruly' publics already assert themselves within health
systems. This book has sought to redress this balance, offering a critical
perspective on participatory practice in public services while acknowledging wider patterns of agency.

The implications of rethinking participation in this way are significant. Invited participation inevitably involves trade-offs and compro-
mises (Learmonth et al., 2009). However, attention should be paid to
making invited spaces welcoming to dissent, even where this makes
the process of participation less comfortable for all concerned. Policy is
inevitably 'unsettled' (Prior and Barnes, 2009), but there is scope for clar-
ification from policymakers on specific points. In the United Kingdom,
the phrase 'public involvement' has allowed two decades of policy to
be produced which holds little shared meaning. Policy should specify

whether it wants the public (or its representatives) to make decisions, to be given the opportunity to express their views on decisions being made by other people, or to do work like conducting consultations or manning hand hygiene stalls. These are vastly different tasks, and there is scope for policymakers to offer a great deal more specification than they hitherto have. Where policy entreats staff to involve 'the public', it should be clearer whether this means simply creating an opportunity for all affected to take part (knowing full well that the vast majority will not), or actually going out and ensuring that the views of the affected (however defined) are heard. More accurately, it should acknowledge that this voice is not simply heard, but is generated, since the public is unlikely to be sitting at home expressing their thoughts on health service management: 'Sometimes, rarely, there is a community voice, clamouring to be heard, but it is usually too angry, resentful, deeply felt, tightly exclusive, or politicised for these programs' (Eliasoph, 2011, p. 252).

Eliciting and channelling these more 'unruly' voices into the governance of healthcare organisations requires a degree of openness to alternative perspectives which is inimical to both highly corporate and highly medicalised decision-making. Public decisions must be genuinely 'up for grabs'. How healthcare organisations treat individuals, whether as worried patients or angry attendees at a public meeting, shapes not just how individuals perceive organisations, but how they come to know their place within them. Acknowledging a more adversarial relationship between a public service and (sections of) its publics – and rejecting the vision of an apathetic public ignoring the 'participatory' opportunities that local institutions offer – might allow us to channel the energies evident in uninvited action into health system decision-making more widely.

References

Abelson, J., 2001. Understanding the role of contextual influences on local health-care decision making: Case study results from Ontario, Canada. *Social Science and Medicine* 53, 777–793(17).

Abelson, J., Forest, P.-G., Eyles, J., Casebeer, A., Mackean, G., 2004. Will it make a difference if I show up and share? A citizens' perspective on improving public involvement processes for health system decision-making. *Journal of Health Services Research and Policy* 9, 205–212.

Abelson, J., Gauvin, F.-P., 2006. Assessing the impacts of public participation: Concepts, evidence and policy implications (No. P 06). Canada Policy Research Networks, Ottawa.

Abu-Lughod, L., 1990. The romance of resistance: Tracing transformations of power through Bedouin women. *American Ethnologist* 17, 41–55. doi:10.1525/ae.1990.17.1.02a00030

Allen, P., Keen, J., Wright, J., Dempster, P., Townsend, J., Hutchings, A., Street, A., Verzulli, R., 2012. Investigating the governance of autonomous public hospitals in England: Multi-site case study of NHS foundation trusts. *Journal of Health Services Research & Policy* 17, 94–100.

Allsop, J., Jones, K., 2008. Withering the citizen, managing the consumer: Complaints in healthcare settings. *Social Policy & Society* 7, 233–243.

Allsop, J., Jones, K., Baggott, R., 2004. Health consumer groups in the UK: A new social movement? *Sociology of Health & Illness* 26, 737–756.

Anderson, W., Florin, D., Gillam, S., Mountford, L., 2002. *Every voice counts: Involving patients and the public in primary care.* King's Fund, London.

Andersson, E., Tritter, J.Q., Wilson, R., 2006. *Healthy democracy: The future of involvement in health and social care.* Involve, London.

Anton, S., McKee, L., Harrison, S., Farrar, S., 2007. Involving the public in NHS service planning. *Journal of Health Organization and Management* 21, 470–483.

Arendt, H., 1998. *The human condition,* 2nd ed. University of Chicago Press, Chicago; London.

Arnett, J.J., 2004. *Emerging adulthood: The winding road from the late teens through the twenties.* Oxford University Press, New York; Oxford.

Arnott, M., Ozga, J., 2010. Nationalism, governance and policymaking in Scotland: The Scottish National Party (SNP) in power. *Public Money & Management* 30, 91–96.

Arnstein, S.R., 1969. A ladder of citizen participation. *Journal of the American Institute of Planners* 35, 216–224.

Aronowitz, R.A., 2012. The rise and fall of the Lyme Disease vaccines: A cautionary tale for risk interventions in American medicine and public health. *Milbank Quarterly* 90, 250–277. doi:10.1111/j.1468-0009.2012.00663.x

Auwaerter, P., Bakken, J., Dattwyler, R., Dumler, J., Halperin, J., McSweegan, E., Nadelman, R., O'Connell, S., Shapiro, E., Sood, S., Steere, A., Weinstein, A., Wormser, G., 2011. Antiscience and ethical concerns associated with advocacy of Lyme disease. *The Lancet Infectious Diseases* 11, 713–719. doi:http://dx.doi. org/10.1016/S1473-3099(11)70034-2

Baggott, R., 2005. A funny thing happened on the way to the forum? Reforming patient and public involvement in the NHS in England. *Public Administration* 83, 533–551.

Bang, H. (2005) Among everyday makers and expert citizens. In Newman, J. (Ed.), Remaking governance: peoples, politics and the public sphere. Bristol: Policy Press.

Barnes, B., 1993. Power, in: Bellamy, R. (Ed.), *Theories and Concepts of Politics: An Introduction.* Manchester University Press, Manchester.

Barnes, M., Newman, J., Knops, A., Sullivan, H., 2003. Constituting 'the public' in public participation. *Public Administration* 81, 379–399.

Barnes, M., Newman, J., Sullivan, H., 2007. *Power, participation and political renewal: Case studies in public participation.* Policy Press, Bristol.

Barnett, R., Barnett, P., 2003. 'If you want to sit on your butts you'll get nothing!' Community activism in response to threats of rural hospital closure in southern New Zealand. *Health & Place* 9, 59–71.

Baxter, J., Hayes, A., Gray, M., 2011. *Families in regional, rural and remote Australia – facts sheet – Australian Institute of Family Studies.* Australian Institute of Family Studies, Melbourne.

BBC News Online, 2007. A&E closure decisions overturned [WWW Document]. URL http://news.bbc.co.uk/1/hi/scotland/6724087.stm (accessed 4.25.13).

Beardwood, B., Walters, V., Eyles, J., French, S., 1999. Complaints against nurses: A reflection of 'the new managerialism' and consumerism in health care? *Social Science & Medicine* 48, 363–374. doi:10.1016/S0277-9536(98)00340-2

Bennet, N., 2014. Health on the agenda in Scottish independence referendum. *The Lancet* 383, 397–398.

Bevir, M., Rhodes, R.A.W., 2006. *Governance stories, Routledge advances in European politics.* Routledge, London.

Birchall, J., 2008. The mutualisation of public services in Britain: A critical commentary. *Journal of Co-operative Studies* 41, 5–16.

Birchall, J., 2001. *The new mutualism in public policy.* Routledge, New York.

Birrell, D., 2009. *The impact of devolution on social policy.* Policy Press, Bristol.

Bishop, P., Davis, G., 2002. Mapping public participation in policy choices. *Australian Journal of Public Administration* 61, 14–29.

Blum, R., Nelson-Mmari, K., 2004. The health of young people in a global context. *Journal of Adolescent Health* 35, 402–418.

BMA Health Policy and Economics Research Unit, 2010. *Devolution – a map of divergence.* BMA, London.

BMA Health Policy and Economics Research Unit, 2007. *Devolution and health policy: A map of divergence within the NHS.* British Medical Association, London.

Bochel, C., Bochel, H., Somerville, P., Worley, C., 2008. Marginalised or enabled voices? 'User participation' in policy and practice. *Social Policy & Society* 7, 201–210.

Boulton, A., Simonsen, K., Walker, T., Cumming, J., Cunningham, C., 2004. Indigenous participation in the 'new' New Zealand health structure. *Journal of Health Services Research & Policy* 9, 35–40.

Bourke, L., Humphreys, J.S., Wakerman, J., Taylor, J., 2012. Understanding rural and remote health: A framework for analysis in Australia. *Health & Place* 18, 496–503. doi:10.1016/j.healthplace.2012.02.009

Braun, K., Schultz, S., 2010. '... a certain amount of engineering involved': Constructing the public in participatory governance arrangements. *Public Understanding of Science* 19, 403–419. doi:10.1177/0963662509347814

Brown, P., 1995. Naming and framing: The social construction of diagnosis and illness. *Journal of Health and Social Behavior* 35, 34–52.

Brown, P., Zavestoski, S., 2004. Social movements in health: An introduction. *Sociology of Health & Illness* 26, 679–694. doi:10.1111/j.0141-9889.2004.00413.x

Brown, T., 2003. Towards an understanding of local protest: Hospital closure and community resistance. *Social & Cultural Geography* 4, 489–506. doi:10.1080/1464936032000137920

Callaghan, G., Wistow, G.D., 2006. Governance and public involvement in the British National Health Service: Understanding difficulties and developments. *Social Science & Medicine* 63, 2289–2300.

Carlyle, E.R., 2013. Sheepdog or watchdog? The role of statutory public involvement institutions in political management of the NHS, 1974–2010 (PhD thesis). Birkbeck, University of London.

Charles, C., Di Maio, S., 1993. Lay participation in health care decision making: A conceptual framework. *Journal of Health Politics, Policy and Law* 18, 881–904.

Church, J., Barker, P., 1998. Regionalization of health services in Canada: A critical perspective. *International Journal of Health Services* 28, 467–486. doi:10.2190/UFPT-7XPW-794C-VJ52

Clarke, J., 2013. In search of ordinary people: The problematic politics of popular participation. *Communication, Culture & Critique* 6, 208–226. doi:10.1111/cccr.12011

Coleman, A.J., Glendinning, C., 2004. Local authority scrutiny of health: Making the views of the community count? *Health Expectations* 7, 29–39.

Conklin, A., Morris, Z., Nolte, E., 2015. What is the evidence base for public involvement in health-care policy?: Results of a systematic scoping review. *Health Expectations* 18, 153–165. doi:10.1111/hex.12038

Conklin, A., Morris, Z.S., Nolte, E., 2010. *Involving the public in healthcare policy: An update of the research evidence and proposed evaluation framework* (Technical Report). RAND Europe, Cambridge.

Contandriopoulos, D., 2004. A sociological perspective on public participation in health care. *Social Science & Medicine* 58, 321–330.

Coote, A., Lenaghan, J., 1997. *Citizens' juries: Theory into practice*. Institute for Public Policy Research, London.

Cornforth, C., 2005. *The governance of public and non-profit organisations: What do boards do?* Taylor & Francis Group, London.

Cornwell, J., 1984. *Hard earned lives: Accounts of health and illness from East London*. Tavistock, London.

Coulter, A., Elwyn, G., 2002. What do patients want from high-quality general practice and how do we involve them in improvement? *British Journal of General Practice* 55, S22–S26.

Crawford, M.J., Rutter, D., Manley, C., Weaver, T., Bhui, K., Fulop, N., Tyrer, P., 2002. Systematic review of involving patients in the planning and development of health care. *British Medical Journal* 325, 1263.

Crawford, M.J., Rutter, D., Thelwall, S., 2003. *User involvement in change management: A review of the literature*. NCCSDO, London.

Curtis, K., Liabo, K., Roberts, H., Barker, M., 2004. Consulted but not heard: A qualitative study of young people's views of their local health service. *Health Expectations* 7, 149–156.

Dalton, R.J., 2008. *The good citizen: How a younger generation is reshaping American politics*. CQ Press, Washington, DC.

Davies, C., Wetherell, M., Barnett, E., 2006. *Citizens at the centre: Deliberative participation in healthcare decisions*. Policy Press, Bristol.

Day, P., Klein, R., 2005. *Governance of foundation trusts: Dilemmas of diversity*. Nuffield Trust, London.

De Certeau, M., 1984. *The practice of everyday life*. University of California Press, Berkeley.

De Certeau, M., Jameson, F., Lovitt, C., 1980. On the oppositional practices of everyday life. *Social Text* 3, 3–43.

Della Porta, D., 2013. Repertoires of contention, in: Snow, D.A., Porta, D.D., Klandermans, B., McAdam, D. *The Wiley-Blackwell Encyclopedia of Social and Political Movements*. Blackwell Publishing Ltd Wiley: Malden, Mass.

Dent, M., 2003. Managing doctors and saving a hospital: Irony, rhetoric and actor networks. *Organization* 10, 107–127. doi:10.1177/1350508403010001379

Edelman, M., 1974. The political language of the helping professions. *Politics and Society* 4, 295–310.

Eliasoph, N., 2011. *Making volunteers: Civic life after welfare's end*. Princeton University Press, Princeton.

Entwistle, V., 2009. Public involvement in health service governance and development: Questions of potential for influence. *Health Expectations* 12, 1–3.

Escobar, O., 2014. *Transformative practices: The political work of public engagement practitioners* (PhD thesis). University of Edinburgh, Edinburgh, UK.

Exworthy, M., Powell, M., Mohan, J., 1999. Markets, bureaucracy and public management: The NHS: Quasi-market, quasi-hierarchy and quasi-network? *Public Money & Management* 19, 15–22. doi:10.1111/1467-9302.00184

Farmer, J., Dawson, P., Martin, E., Tucker, J., 2007. Rurality, remoteness and the change process: Evidence from a study of maternity services in the north of Scotland. *Health Services Management Research* 20, 59–68. doi:10.1258/095148407779614963

Farrell, C., 2004. *Patient and public involvement in health: The evidence for policy implementation*. Department of Health, London.

Feingold, E., 1977. Citizen participation: A review of the issues, in: Rosen, H., Levey, S., Metsch, J. (Eds), *The Consumer and the Health Care System: Social and Managerial Perspectives*. Spectrum Publications, New York.

Felt, U., Fochler, M., 2010. Machineries for making publics: Inscribing and de-scribing publics in public engagement. *Minerva* 48, 219–238.

Felt, U., Fochler, M., 2008. The bottom-up meanings of the concept of public participation in science and technology. *Science and Public Policy* 35, 489–499. doi:10.3152/030234208X329086

FMR Research, 2008. *Public partnership forums: What direction and support is needed for the future?* Scottish Health Council, Glasgow.

Fontana, L., 1988. Health planning and the closure of a community hospital. *The International Journal of Health Planning and Management* 3, 273–89. doi:10.1002/hpm.4740030406

Foot, M., 2009. *Aneurin Bevan: A Biography: Volume 2: 1945–1960*. Faber & Faber, London.

Forbat, L., Hubbard, G., Kearney, N., 2009. Patient and public involvement: Models and muddles. *Journal of Clinical Nursing* 18, 2547–2554.

Forster, R., Gabe, J., 2008. Voice or choice? Patient and public involvement in the National Health Service in England under New Labour. *International Journal of Health Services* 38, 333–356.

Fox, S., Rainie, L., 2002. E-patients and the online health care revolution. *Physician Executive* 28, 14–17.

Fraser, J., 2004. A case report: Ethics of a proposed qualitative study of hospital closure in an Australian rural community. *Family Practice* 21, 87–91. doi:10.1093/fampra/cmh119

Freeman, R., 2009. What is translation? *Evidence & Policy* 5, 429–447.

Freeman, R., 2008. Learning by meeting. *Critical Policy Studies* 2, 1–24. doi:10.10 80/19460171.2008.9518529

Freeman, R., 2006. The work the document does: Research, policy and equity in health. *Journal of Health Politics, Policy and Law* 31, 51–70.

Freeman, R., Sturdy, S., 2014. *Knowledge in policy: Embodied, inscribed, enacted*. Policy Press, Bristol.

Freeman, T., Baum, F.E., Jolley, G.M., Lawless, A., Edwards, T., Javanparast, S., Ziersch, A., 2014. Service providers' views of community participation at six Australian primary healthcare services: Scope for empowerment and challenges to implementation. *International Journal of Health Planning and Management Early View*. doi:10.1002/hpm.2253

Freud, S., 1961. *Civilisation and its discontents*. W.W. Norton, London.

Fulop, N., Walters, R., Perri6, Spurgeon, P., 2012. Implementing changes to hospital services: Factors influencing the process and 'results' of reconfiguration. *Health Policy* 104, 128–135. doi:10.1016/j.healthpol.2011.05.015

Furlong, A., Cartmel, F., 2007. *Young people and social change: New perspectives, Sociology and social change*, 2nd ed. Open University Press, Maidenhead.

Gauld, R., 2005. Delivering democracy? An analysis of New Zealand's District Health Board elections, 2001 and 2004. *Australian Health Review* 29, 345.

Gaventa, J., 2006. Finding the spaces for change: A power analysis. *IDS Bulletin* 37, 23–33.

Gerdvilaite, J., Nachtnebel, A., 2011. Disinvestment. Overview of disinvestment experiences and challenges in selected countries (Project Report).

Gibson, A., Britten, N., Lynch, J., 2012. Theoretical directions for an emancipatory concept of patient and public involvement. *Health (London)* 16, 531–547. doi:10.1177/1363459312438563

Gifford, B., Mullner, R., 1988. Modeling hospital closure relative to organizational theory – the applicability of ecology theory's environmental determinism and adaptation perspectives. *Social Science & Medicine* 27, 1287–1294. doi:10.1016/0277-9536(88)90359-0

Gorsky, M., Mohan, J., Willis, T., 2005. From hospital contributory schemes to health cash plans: The mutual idea in British health care after 1948. *Journal of Social Policy* 34, 447–467.

Greener, I., 2009. Towards a history of choice in UK health policy. *Sociology of Health & Illness* 31, 309–324.

Greener, I., 2008. Choice and voice – a review. *Social Policy & Society* 7, 255–265.

Greener, I., 2002. Understanding NHS reform: The policy-transfer, social learning, and path-dependency perspectives. *Governance* 15, 161–183. doi:10.1111/1468-0491.00184

Greenhalgh, T., 1999. Narrative based medicine in an evidence based world. *BMJ* 318, 323–325.

Greenhalgh, T., Robert, G., Macfarlane, F., Bate, P., Kyriakidou, O., Peacock, R., 2005. Storylines of research in diffusion of innovation: A meta-narrative approach to systematic review. *Social Science & Medicine* 61, 417–430.

Greer, S.L., 2004. *Territorial politics and health policy : UK health policy in comparative perspective, Devolution series*. Manchester University Press, Manchester.

Greer, S.L., Donnelly, P.D., Wilson, I., Stewart, E.A., 2012. *Health board elections and alternative pilots: Final report of the statutory evaluation*. The Scottish Government, Edinburgh.

Greer, S.L., Donnelly, P.D., Wilson, I., Stewart, E.A., 2011. *Health board elections and alternative pilots in NHS Scotland: Interim evaluation report*. Scottish Government Social Research, Edinburgh.

Greer, S.L., Stewart, E.A., Wilson, I., Donnelly, P.D., 2014a. Victory for volunteerism? Scottish health board elections and participation in the welfare state. *Social Science & Medicine* 106, 221–228. doi:10.1016/j.socscimed.2014.01.053

Greer, S.L., Wilson, I., Stewart, E., Donnelly, P.D., 2014b. 'Democratizing' public services? Representation and elections in the Scottish NHS. *Public Administration* 92, 1090–1105. doi:10.1111/padm.12101

Greer, S.L., Trench, A., 2010. Health and intergovernmental relations in the devolved United Kingdom. *Policy & Politics* 38, 509–529.

Haas, M.R., Hall, J.P., Chinchen, L.A., 2001. The moving of St Vincent's: A tale in two cities. *Medical Journal of Australia* 174, 93–96.

Hagen, T.P., Vrangbaek, K., 2009. The changing political governance structures of Nordic health care systems, in: Magnussen, J., Vrangbaek, K., and Saltman, R.B. *Nordic Health Care Systems: Recent Reforms and Current Policy Challenges, European Observatory on Health Systems and Policies*. Open University Press, Maidenhead.

Ham, C., 2009. *Health in a cold climate: Developing an intelligent response to the financial challenges facing the NHS*. Nuffield Trust, London.

Ham, C., 1980. Community Health Council participation in the NHS planning system. *Social Policy & Administration* 14, 221–232.

Harre, N., 2007. Community service or activism as an identity project for youth. *Journal of Community Psychology* 35, 711–724.

Harrington, B.E., Smith, K.E., Hunter, D.J., Marks, L., Blackman, T.J., McKee, L., Greene, A., Elliott, E., Williams, G.H., 2009. Health inequalities in England, Scotland and Wales: Stakeholders' accounts and policy compared. *Public Health* 123, e24–e28.

Harrison, S., Dowswell, G., Milewa, T., 2002. Guest editorial: Public and user 'involvement' in the UK National Health Service. *Health & Social Care in the Community* 10, 63–66.

Harrison, S., McDonald, R., 2008. *The politics of healthcare in Britain*. Sage, Los Angeles; London.

Harrison, S., Mort, M., 1998. Which champions, which people? Public and user involvement in health care as a technology of legitimation. *Social Policy and Administration* 32, 60–70(11).

Health Boards (Membership and Elections) (Scotland) Act, 2009 (asp 5). Available at http://www.legislation.gov.uk/asp/2009/5/section/1.

Heaton, J., Sloper, P., Clarke, S., 2007. Access to and use of NHS Patient Advice and Liaison Service (PALS): The views of children, young people, parents and PALS staff. *Child: Care, Health and Development* 30, 495–501.

Hirschman, A.O., 1970. *Exit, voice, and loyalty: Responses to decline in firms, organizations, and States.* Harvard University Press, Cambridge, MA; London.

Hogg, C., Williamson, C., 2001. Whose interests do lay people represent? Towards an understanding of the role of lay people as members of committees. *Health Expectations* 4, 2–9.

House of Commons – Health Committee, 2007. *Public and patient involvement in the NHS: Third report of session 2006–7 (No. HC 278-I).* The Stationery Office, London.

Huby, G., 1997. Interpreting silence, documenting experience: An anthropological approach to the study of health service users' experience with HIV/AIDS care in Lothian, Scotland. *Social Science & Medicine* 44, 1149–1160.

Hudson, B., 1998. Circumstances change cases: Local government and the NHS. *Social Policy & Administration* 32, 71–86.

Hunter, D.J., Harrison, S., 1997. Democracy, accountability and consumerism, in: Munro, J., Iliffe, S. (Eds), *Healthy Choices: Future Options for the NHS.* Lawrence & Wishart, London.

Ingram, H., Schneider, A.L., 2007. Policy analysis for democracy, in: Fischer, F., Miller, G., Sidney, M.S. (Eds), *Handbook of Public Policy Analysis: Theory, Politics, and Methods.* CRC/Taylor & Francis, Boca Raton.

James, A.M., 1999. Closing rural hospitals in Saskatchewan: On the road to wellness? *Social Science & Medicine* 49, 1021–1034.

Jones, K., Baggott, R., Allsop, J., 2004. Influencing the national policy process: The role of health consumer groups. *Health Expectations* 7, 18–28.

Katikireddi, S.V., McKee, M., Craig, P., Stuckler, D., 2014. The NHS reforms in England: Four challenges to evaluating success and failure. *Journal of the Royal Society of Medicine* 107, 387–392. doi:10.1177/0141076814550358

Keating, M., 2010. *The government of Scotland: Public policy making after devolution,* 2nd ed. Edinburgh University Press, Edinburgh.

Keating, M., 2002. Devolution and public policy in the United Kingdom: Divergence or convergence?, in: Robinson, P., Adams, J. (Eds), *Devolution in Practice: Public Policy Differences within the UK.* IPPR, London.

Keating, M., Stevenson, L., Cairney, P., MacLean, K., 2003. Does devolution make a difference? Legislative output and policy divergence in Scotland. *Journal of Legislative Studies* 9, 110–139.

King, S., 2004. Pink Ribbons Inc: Breast cancer activism and the politics of philanthropy. *International Journal of Qualitative Studies in Education* 17, 473–492.

Kirouac-Fram, J., 2010. 'To serve the community best': Reconsidering Black politics in the struggle to save Homer G. Phillips Hospital in St. Louis, 1976–1984. *Journal of Urban History* 36(5), 594–616.

Klein, R., 2010. *The new politics of the NHS: From creation to reinvention,* 6th ed. Radcliffe, Oxford.

Klein, R., 2004. Too much of a good thing? Over-investing in public involvement in the NHS. *New Economy* 11, 207–212.

Klein, R., Lewis, J., 1976. *The politics of consumer representation: A study of community health councils.* Centre for Studies in Social Policy, London.

Klein, R., New, B., 1998. *Two cheers? Reflections on the health of NHS democracy.* King's Fund Publishing, London.

Klijn, E.H., Skelcher, C., 2007. Democracy and governance networks: Compatible or not? *Public Administration* 85, 587–608.

Kuhn, T.S., 1962. *The structure of scientific revolutions, international encyclopaedia of unified science;* v. 2, no. 2. University of Chicago Press, Chicago.

Latour, B., 2005. From Realpolitik to Dingpolitik or how to make things public, in: Latour, B., Weibel, P. (Eds), *Making Things Public : Atmospheres of Democracy.* MIT Press: ZKM/Center for Art and Media in Karlsruhe, Cambridge, MA; Karlsruhe, Germany.

Laugesen, M., Gauld, R., 2012. Democratic governance and health: Hospitals, politics and health policy in New Zealand. Otago University Press, Dunedin, New Zealand.

Leadbetter, C., 2004. *Personalisation through participation: A new script for public services.* Demos, London.

Learmonth, M., Martin, G.P., Warwick, P., 2009. Ordinary and effective: The Catch-22 in managing the public voice in health care? *Health Expectations* 12, 106–115.

Le Grand, J., 2007. *The other invisible hand: Delivering public services through choice and competition.* Princeton University Press, Princeton.

Le Grand, J., 1991. Quasi-markets and social policy. *The Economic Journal* 101, 1256–1267.

Lehoux, P., Daudelin, G., Abelson, J., 2012. The unbearable lightness of citizens within public deliberation processes. *Social Science & Medicine* 74, 1843–1850. doi:10.1016/j.socscimed.2012.02.023

Lepnurm, R., Lepnurm, M.K., 2001. The closure of rural hospitals in Saskatchewan: Method or madness? *Social Science & Medicine* 52, 1689–1707. doi:10.1016/S0277-9536(00)00283-5

Liddell, G., Burnside, R., Campbell, A., McGrath, F., McIver, I., 2012. Local government elections 2012 (SPICe Briefing No. 12/38). Edinburgh, Scottish Parliament Information Centre.

Lightfoot, J., Sloper, P., 2006. Having a say in health: Involving young people with a chronic illness or physical disability in local health services. *Children & Society* 17, 277–290.

Lindbom, A., 2014. Waking up the giant? Hospital closures and electoral punishment in Sweden, in: Kumlin, S., Stadelmann-Steffen, I. (Eds), *How Welfare States Shape the Democratic Public: Policy Feedback, Participation, Voting, and Attitudes.* Edward Elgar, Cheltenham, UK; Northampton, MA.

Li, T.M., 2007. Practices of assemblage and community forest management. *Economy and Society* 36, 263–293.

Litva, A., Canvin, K., Shepherd, M., Jacoby, A., Gabbay, M., 2009. Lay perceptions of the desired role and type of user involvement in clinical governance. *Health Expectations* 12, 81–91.

Litva, A., Coast, J., Donovan, J., Eyles, J., Shepherd, M., Tacchi, J., Abelson, J., Morgan, K., 2002. 'The public is too subjective': Public involvement at different levels of health-care decision making. *Social Science and Medicine* 54, 1825–1837.

Locker, D., 1981. *Symptoms and illness: The cognitive organisation of disorder.* Tavistock Publications, London.

Lorde, A., 2012. *Sister outsider: Essays and speeches.* Potter/TenSpeed/Harmony.

Lupton, D., 2014. The commodification of patient opinion: The digital patient experience economy in the age of big data. *Sociology of Health & Illness* 36, 856–869.

Mack, L., 2010. Community advisory committees: Drivers of consumer, carer, and community participation in Victoria's public health services. *The Journal of Ambulatory Care Management* 33, 198–204. doi:10.1097/JAC.0b013e3181e5ebf2

Macpherson, S., 2008. Reaching the top of the ladder? Locating the voices of excluded young people within the participation debate. *Policy and Politics* 36, 361–379.

Magnussen, J., Vrangbaek, K., Saltman, R.B., 2009. *Nordic health care systems: Recent reforms and current policy challenges, European observatory on health systems and policies.* Open University Press, Maidenhead.

Mahony, N., Newman, J., Barnett, C., 2010. *Rethinking the public: Innovations in research, theory and politics.* Policy Press, Bristol.

Mann, C., Voß, J.-P., Amelung, N., Simons, A., Runge, T., Grabner, L. (2013) Challenging futures of citizen panels: a report based on an interactive, anticipatory assessment of the dynamics of governance instruments. Berlin: Technische Universitat Berlin.

Marsh, D., O'Toole, T., Jones, S., 2007. *Young people and politics in the UK: Apathy or alienation?* Palgrave Macmillan, Basingstoke.

Martin, G.P., 2008a. Representativeness, legitimacy and power in public involvement in health-care management. *Social Science & Medicine* 67, 1757–1765.

Martin, G.P., 2008b. 'Ordinary people only': Knowledge, representativeness, and the publics of public participation in healthcare. *Sociology of Health & Illness* 30, 35–54.

Martin, S., 2009. Engaging with citizens and other stakeholders, in: Bovaird, T., Loffler, E. (Eds), *Public Management and Governance.* Routledge, London.

Martinussen, P.E., Magnussen, J., 2009. Health care reform: The Nordic experience, in: Magnussen, J., Vrangbaek, K., and Saltman, R.B. *Nordic Health Care Systems: Recent Reforms and Current Policy Challenges, European Observatory on Health Systems and Policies.* Open University Press, Maidenhead.

McAra, L., 2008. Crime, criminology and criminal justice in Scotland. *European Journal of Criminology* 5, 481–504. doi:10.1177/1477370808095127

McCoy, L., 2006. Keeping the institution in view: Working with interview accounts of everyday experience, in: Smith, D.E. *Institutional Ethnography as Practice.* Rowman & Littlefield, Oxford.

McGarvey, N., Cairney, P., 2008. *Scottish politics: An introduction.* Palgrave Macmillan, Basingstoke.

McKissock, K., 2008. *Better together: Scotland's patient experience programme. Public priorities with respect to general practice care (No. No.3/2008).* The Scottish Government, Edinburgh.

McPherson, A., Raab, C.D., 1988. *Governing education: A sociology of policy since 1945.* Edinburgh University Press, Edinburgh.

Meuleman, B., Boushel, C., 2014. Hashtags, ruling relations and the everyday: Institutional ethnography insights on social movements. *Contemporary Social Science* 9, 49–62.

Mitton, C., Smith, N., Peacock, S., Evoy, B., Abelson, J., 2009. Public participation in health care priority setting: A scoping review. *Health Policy* 91, 219–228.

Mockford, C., Staniszewska, S., Griffiths, F., Herron-Marx, S., 2012. The impact of patient and public involvement on UK NHS health care: A systematic review. *International Journal for Quality in Health Care* 24, 28–38. doi:10.1093/intqhc/mzr066

Moini, G., 2011. How participation has become a hegemonic discursive resource: Towards an interpretivist research agenda. *Critical Policy Studies* 5, 149–168. doi :10.1080/19460171.2011.576524

Mol, A., 2008. *The logic of care: Health and the problem of patient choice*. Routledge, London; New York.

Mol, A., 2006. Proving or improving: On health care research as a form of self-reflection. *Qualitative Health Research* 16, 405.

Mooney, G., Poole, L., 2004. 'A land of milk and honey'? Social policy in Scotland after devolution. *Critical Social Policy* 24, 458.

Mooney, G., Scott, G., 2005. *Exploring social policy in the 'new' Scotland*. Policy Press, Bristol.

Moon, G., Brown, T., 2001. Closing Barts: Community and resistance in contemporary UK hospital policy. *Environment and Planning D: Society and Space* 19, 43–59. doi:10.1068/d35j

Mullen, C., Hughes, D., Vincent-Jones, P., 2011. The democratic potential of public participation: Healthcare governance in England. *Social & Legal Studies* 20, 21–38. doi:10.1177/0964663910391349

Mungall, I., 2004. Trend towards centralisation of hospital services, and its effect on access to care for rural and remote communities in the UK. *Rural Remote Health* 5, 390–390.

National Framework Advisory Group, 2005. *Building a health service fit for the future: A national framework for service change in the NHS in Scotland*. Scottish Executive, Edinburgh.

Needham, C., 2009. Interpreting personalization in England's National Health Service: A textual analysis. *Critical Policy Studies* 3, 204–220.

Nettleton, S., Burrows, R., 2003. E-Scaped Medicine? Information, Reflexivity and Health. *Critical Social Policy* 23, 165–185. doi:10.1177/0261018303023002003

Newman, J., Clarke, J., 2009. *Publics, politics and power: Remaking the public in public services*. Sage, London; Thousand Oaks, CA.

Norris, P., 2002. *Democratic phoenix: Reinventing political activism*. Cambridge University Press, Cambridge.

Oborn, E., 2008. Legitimacy of hospital reconfiguration: The controversial downsizing of Kidderminster hospital. *Journal of Health Services Research & Policy* 13 Suppl 2, 11–18. doi:10.1258/jhsrp.2007.007093

O'Donovan, O., Moreira, T., Howlett, E., 2013. Tracking Transformations in Health Movement Organisations: Alzheimer's Disease Organisations and their Changing 'Cause Regimes'. *Social Movement Studies* 12, 316–334.

O'Keefe, E., Hogg, C., 1999. Public participation and marginalised groups: The community development model. *Health Expectations* 2, 245–254.

Parry, R., 2002. Delivery structures and policy development in post-devolution Scotland. *Social Policy & Society* 1, 315–324.

Pateman, C., 1976. *Participation and democratic theory*. Cambridge University Press, Cambridge.

Patterson, P.M., 2000. The talking cure and the silent treatment: Some limits of 'discourse' as speech. *Administrative Theory & Praxis* 22, 663–695.

Pattie, C., Seyd, P., Whiteley, P., 2004. *Citizenship in Britain: Values, participation, and democracy.* Cambridge University Press, Cambridge.

Peckham, S., Exworthy, M., Greener, I., Powell, M., 2005. Decentralizing health services: More local accountability or just more central control? *Public Money & Management* 25, 221–228. doi:10.1080/09540962.2005.10600097

Peckham, S., Mays, N., Hughes, D., Sanderson, M., Allen, P., Prior, L., Entwistle, V., Thompson, A., Davies, H., 2012. Devolution and patient choice: Policy rhetoric versus experience in practice. *Social Policy & Administration* 46, 199–218.

Philips, H., Remmen, R., Paepe, P.D., Buylaert, W., Royen, P.V., 2010. Out of hours care: A profile analysis of patients attending the emergency department and the general practitioner on call. *BMC Family Practice* 11, 88. doi:10.1186/1471-2296-11-88

Pickard, S., 1997. The future organization of community health councils. *Social Policy & Administration* 31, 247–289.

Pitkin, H.F., 1981. Justice: On relating private and public. *Political Theory* 9, 327–352.

Pitkin, H.F., 1967. *The concept of representation.* University of California Press, Berkeley.

Piven, F.F., Cloward, R.A., 1972. *Regulating the poor: The functions of public welfare, Studies in social ecology and pathology.* Tavistock Publications, London.

Polletta, F., 2014. Is participation without power good enough? Introduction to 'Democracy Now: Ethnographies of Contemporary Participation'. *The Sociological Quarterly* 55, 453–466. doi:10.1111/tsq.12062

Pollitt, C., 2008. *Time, policy, management: Governing with the past: Governing with the past.* Oxford University Press, Oxford.

Prior, D., 2009. Policy, power and the potential for counter-agency, in: Barnes, M., Prior, D. (Eds), *Subversive Citizens: Power, Agency and Resistance in Public Services.* Policy Press, England.

Prior, D., Barnes, M., 2011. Subverting social policy on the front line: Agencies of resistance in the delivery of services. *Social Policy & Administration* 45, 264–279. doi:10.1111/j.1467-9515.2011.00768.x

Prior, D., Barnes, M., 2009. 'Subversion' and the analysis of public policy, in: Barnes, M., Prior, D. (Eds), *Subversive Citizens: Power, Agency and Resistance in Public Services.* Policy Press, England.

Prior, L., Hughes, D., Peckham, S., 2012. The discursive turn in policy analysis and the validation of policy stories. *Journal of Social Policy* 41, 271–289.

Rabeharisoa, V., Moreira, T., Akrich, M., 2014. Evidence-based activism: Patients', users' and activists' groups in knowledge society. *BioSocieties* 9, 111–128. doi:10.1057/biosoc.2014.2

Reda, S., 1996. Public opinions about preparation required before closing psychiatric hospitals. *Journal of Mental Health* 5, 407–420.

Reeves, R., 2008. *Better together: Scotland's patient experience programme building on the experiences of NHS boards (Research findings No. No.1/2008), Social research.* The Scottish Government, Edinburgh.

Remote and Rural Steering Group, 2007. *Delivering for remote and rural healthcare.* NHS Scotland, Edinburgh.

Rhodes, R.A.W., 1997. *Understanding governance: Policy networks, governance, reflexivity and accountability, Public policy and management.* Open University Press, Buckingham.

Riley, S.C.E., Griffin, C., Morey, Y., 2010. The case for 'everyday politics': Evaluating neo-tribal theory as a way to understand alternative forms of political participation, using electronic dance music culture as an example. *Sociology* 44, 345–363. doi:10.1177/0038038509357206

Roberts, J.M., Devine, F., 2004. Some everyday experiences of voluntarism: Social capital, pleasure, and the contingency of participation. *Social Politics: International Studies in Gender, State & Society* 11, 280–296. doi:10.1093/sp/jxh036

Rowe, G., Frewer, L.J., 2005. A typology of public engagement mechanisms. *Science, Technology & Human Values* 30, 251–290. doi:10.1177/0162243904271724

Ruane, S., 2011. Save our hospital campaigns in England: Why do some hospital campaigns succeed?, in: Lister, J. (Ed.), *Europe's Health for Sale: The Heavy Cost of Privatisation.* Libri Publishing, Southampton.

Russell, A., 2007. Youth and political engagement, in: Russell, A., Stoker, G. (Eds), *Failing Politics? A Response to the Governance of Great Britain Green Paper.* Political Studies Association, Newcastle.

Sartori, G., 1984. *Social science concepts: A systematic analysis.* Sage Publications, Beverly Hills, CA.

Sartori, G., 1970. Concept misformation in comparative politics. *The American Political Science Review* 64, 1033–1053.

Scambler, G., 2001. *Habermas, critical theory and health.* Routledge, New York.

Scambler, G., Britten, N., 2001. System, lifeworld and doctor-patient interaction: Issues of trust in a changing world, in: Scambler, G. (Ed.), *Habermas, Critical Theory and Health.* Routledge, New York, pp. viii, 212.

Schegloff, E.A., 2005. On complainability. *Social Problems* 52, 449–476.

Schneider, A.L., Ingram, H., 1990. Behavioural assumptions of policy tools. *Journal of Politics* 52, 510–539.

Scott, J.C., 1990. *Domination and the arts of resistance: Hidden transcripts.* Yale University Press, New Haven; London.

Scottish Council Foundation, McCormick-McDowell, 2008. *Function and Form: An independent review of the Scottish Health Council.* Scottish Council Foundation, Edinburgh.

Scottish Executive, 2005. *Delivering for health.* Scottish Executive, Edinburgh.

Scottish Executive, 2004. *Community health partnerships: Involving people advice notes.* Scottish Executive, Edinburgh.

Scottish Executive, 2003. *Partnership for care.* Scottish Executive, Edinburgh.

Scottish Executive, 2001. *Patient focus and public involvement.* Scottish Executive, Edinburgh.

Scottish Executive, 2000. *Our national health – a plan for action, a plan for change* The Scottish Executive: Edinburgh.

Scottish Government, 2012. *Rural Scotland key facts 2012.* The Scottish Government, Edinburgh.

Scottish Health Council, 2010. *A participation standard for the NHS in Scotland.* Scottish Health Council, Glasgow.

Scottish Health Council, 2009. *Action plan: A form fit to function.* Scottish Health Council, Glasgow.

Skelcher, C., 1998. *The appointed state: Quasi-governmental organizations and democracy.* Open University Press, Maidenhead.

Skelton, T., Valentine, G., 2003. Political participation, political action and political identities: Young D/deaf people's perspectives. *Space and Polity* 7, 117–134.

Smith, D.E., 2005. Institutional ethnography: A sociology for people. AltaMira Press, Lanham, MD.

Smith, D.E., 2001. Texts and the ontology of organisations and institutions. *Studies in Cultures, Organisations and Societies* 7, 159–198.

Smith, D.E., 1999. From women's standpoint to a sociology for people, in: Abu-Loghod, J.L. *Sociology for the Twenty-First Century: Continuities and Cutting Edges.* University of Chicago Press, Chicago, IL.

Smith, G., 2005. *Beyond the ballot: 57 democratic innovations from around the world.* Power Inquiry, London.

Smith, K.E., Hunter, D.J., Blackman, T., Elliott, E., Greene, A., Harrington, B.E., Marks, L., McKee, L., Williams, G.H., 2009. Divergence or convergence? Health inequalities and policy in a devolved Britain. *Critical Social Policy* 29, 216–242.

Soss, J., 2006. Talking our way to meaningful explanations, in: Schwartz-Shea, P., Yanow, D. (Eds), *Interpretation and Method: Empirical Research Methods and the Interpretive Turn.* M.E. Sharpe, Armonk, NY.

Soss, J., 2000. *Unwanted claims: The politics of participation in the US welfare system.* The University of Michigan Press, Ann Arbor.

South, J., 2007. A critical analysis of the development of the Patient Advice and Liaison Service (PALS). *Journal of Health Organization and Management* 21, 149–165.

Statistics Canada, 2011. *Canada's rural population since 1851.* Statistics Canada.

Statistics New Zealand, 2002. *New Zealand: An urban/rural profile.* Statistics New Zealand, Wellington, NZ.

Stewart, E.A., 2015. Seeking outsider perspectives in interpretive research: young adults and citizen participation in health policy. *Critical Policy Studies*, 9(2), 198–215.

Stewart, E.A., 2013. A mutual NHS? The emergence of distinctive public involvement policy in a devolved Scotland. *Policy & Politics* 41, 241–259. doi:http://dx.doi.org/10.1332/030557312X655404

Stewart, E.A., 2012. *Governance, participation and avoidance: Everyday public involvement in the Scottish NHS (PhD thesis).* University of Edinburgh, Edinburgh.

Stewart, E.A., Greer, S.L., Wilson, I., Donnelly, P.D., 2015. Power to the people? An international review of the democratizing effects of direct elections to healthcare organizations. *International Journal of Health Planning and Management Early View* DOI: 10.1002/hpm.2282.

Stewart, E.A., Wilson, I., Donnelly, P.D., Greer, S.L., 2014. 'I didn't have a clue what we were doing': (Not) engaging 16 and 17 year old Voters in Scotland. *Scottish Affairs* 23, 354–368. doi:10.3366/scot.2014.0034

Sullivan, H., 2009. Subversive spheres: Neighbourhoods, citizens and the 'new governance', in: Barnes, M., Prior, D. (Eds), *Subversive Citizens: Power, Agency and Resistance in Public Services.* Policy Press, England.

Taghizadeh, J.L., Lindbom, A., 2014. Protests against welfare retrenchment: Healthcare restructuring in Sweden. *Scandinavian Political Studies* 37, 1–20.

Tannahill, C., 2005. Health and health policy, in: Mooney, G., Scott, G. (Eds), *Exploring Social Policy in the 'New' Scotland.* Policy Press, Bristol.

Tenbensel, T., 2010. Virtual special issue introduction: Public participation in high income countries – a review of why, who, what, which, where? *Social Science & Medicine* 71, 1537–1540.

The Scottish Government, 2009. News release: Elected health boards get go-ahead [WWW Document]. URL http://www.scotland.gov.uk/News/Releases/2009/03/12171601 (accessed 1.1.14).

The Scottish Government, 2007. *Better health, better care.* Scottish Government: Edinburgh.

The Tavistock Institute, Involve, Demsoc, Public-I, 2014. NHS citizen assembly team learning report [WWW Document]. URL http://www.nhscitizen.org.uk/wp-content/uploads/2014/08/Assembly-Learning-Report.pdf (accessed 3.22.15).

Thomson, E., Farmer, J., Tucker, J., Bryers, H., 2008. Informing debate or fuelling dispute? Media communication of reconfiguration in Scotland's rural maternity care. *Social Policy & Administration* 42, 789–812. doi:http://dx.doi.org.ezproxy.is.ed.ac.uk/10.1111/j.1467-9515.2008.00638.x

Tilly, C., 1986. *The contentious French.* Belknap Press of Harvard University Press, Cambridge, MA.

Tilly, C., Tarrow, S., 2006. *Contentious politics.* Oxford University Press.

Tritter, J.Q., 2009. Revolution or evolution: The challenges of conceptualising patient and public involvement in a consumerist world. *Health Expectations* 12, 275–287.

Tritter, J.Q., McCallum, A., 2006. The snakes and ladders of user involvement: Moving beyond Arnstein. *Health Policy* 76, 156–168.

UK Parliament, 2011. Glossary of parliamentary terms [WWW Document]. URL http://www.parliament.uk/site-information/glossary/ (accessed 1.1.01).

UNISON Scotland, 2008. UNISON Scotland health boards (Membership and elections) response [WWW Document]. URL http://www.unison-scotland.org.uk/response/healthboards.html (accessed 3.31.15).

Urbinati, N., Warren, M.E., 2008. The concept of representation in contemporary democratic theory. *Annual Review of Political Science* 11, 387–412. doi:10.1146/annurev.polisci.11.053006.190533

Veronesi, G., Keasey, K., 2011. National health service boards of directors and governance models. *Public Management Review* 13, 861–885. doi:10.1080/14719037.2010.539113

Veronesi, G., Keasey, K., 2010. NHS boards: Knowing the 'what' but not the 'how'. *Public Money & Management* 30, 363–370. doi:10.1080/09540962.2010.525005

Vickers, G., 1965. *The art of judgement: A study of policy making.* Harper & Row, London.

Voß, J.-P., 2015. Reflexively engaging with technologies of participation: constructive assessment for public participation methods, in: Chilvers, J., Kearnes, M.B. (Eds), Remaking participation: science, environment and emergent publics. Routledge-Earthscan, London.

Wagenaar, H., 2011. *Meaning in action: Interpretation and dialogue in policy analysis.* M.E. Sharpe, Armonk, NY; London.

Wait, S., Nolte, E., 2006. Public involvement policies in health: Exploring their conceptual basis. *Health Economics, Policy and Law* 1, 149–162. doi:10.1017/S174413310500112X

Ward, J., McMurray, R., 2011. The unspoken work of general practitioner receptionists: A re-examination of emotion management in primary care. *Social
Science & Medicine* 72, 1583–1587.

Warren, M.E., 2009a. Citizen participation and democratic deficits: Considerations
from the perspective of democratic theory, in: DeBardeleben, J., Pammett, J.H.
(Eds), *Activating the Citizen: Dilemmas of Participation in Europe and Canada*.
Palgrave Macmillan, Basingstoke.

Warren, M.E., 2009b. Governance-driven democratization. *Critical Policy Studies*
3, 3–13.

Warren, M.E., 1996. What should we expect from more democracy? Radically
democratic responses to politics. *Political Theory* 24, 241–270.

Weiss, R.S., 1994. *Learning from strangers: The art and method of qualitative interview
studies*. The Free Press, New York.

Williams, R., 1976. *Keywords: A vocabulary of culture and society*. Fontana, London.

Wilson, I., Greer, S.L., Stewart, E., Donnelly, P., 2015. Turnout, information and
heuristics in the Scottish Health Board Elections: 'getting a CV with no job
description'. *Political Studies Early View*. DOI: 10.1111/1467-9248.12184.

Wiseman, V., Mooney, G., Berry, G., Tang, K.C., 2003. Involving the general
public in priority setting: Experiences from Australia. *Social Science and Medicine*
56, 1001–1012.

Wittgenstein, L., 1953. *Philosophical investigations*. B. Blackwell, Oxford.

World Health Organisation, 1978. *Declaration of Ama-Ata*. Presented at the
International Conference on Primary Health Care.

Wyke, S., 2003. Why people use primary care services. Do we really need more
research? *Journal of Health Services Research and Policy* 8, 55–56.

Wynne, B., 2007. Public participation in Science and Technology: Performing
and obscuring a political-conceptual category mistake. *East Asian Science,
Technology and Society: An International Journal* 1, 99–110.

Yanow, D., 2000. *Conducting interpretive policy analysis, qualitative research methods*. Sage Publications, Thousand Oaks, CA; London.

Yanow, D., 1996. *How does a policy mean? Interpreting policy and organizational
actions*. Georgetown University Press, Washington, DC.

Index

CPSIA information can be obtained
at www.ICGtesting.com
Printed in the USA
LVOW01*1505120516
487958LV00015B/233/P